Eyewitness Accounts of the American Revolution

Travels Through the Interior Parts of America

Thomas Anburey

The New York Times & Arno Press

T R A V E L S

THROUGH THE

INTERIOR PARTS

OF

A M E R I C A.

IN A

SERIES OF LETTERS.

BY AN OFFICER.

Τί ἔν, ἄν τις εἴποι, ταῦτα λέγεις ἡμῖν νῦν;
Ἵνα γνῶτε, καὶ αἴσθησθε ἀμφότερα.

DEMOSTH. OLYNTH.

VOL. I.

LONDON:
Printed for WILLIAM LANE, Leadenhall-Street.
MDCCLXXXIX.

EARL OF HARRINGTON,

VISCOUNT PETERSHAM,

AND

COLONEL OF THE TWENTY-NINTH-REGIMENT OF FOOT.

MY LORD,

HAVING had the honor to ſerve under your Lordſhip, it was my fortune, in common with all who were in the ſame ſitua-

fituation, to become attached to your Lordfhip by perfonal obligations; and it is a confequence which I hope will be thought equally natural, that I fhould take this occàfion to acknowledge them.

In laying before the Public uncommon fcenes of difficulty, danger and diftrefs, I might be further tempted, had I talents for the undertaking, to particularize the unremitting fortitude, which, in feveral of the moft trying inftances, diftinguifhed your Lordfhip's conduct: but examples of bravery, though none can be more confpicuous than thofe your Lord fhip fhewed, abound in every clafs of a Britifh army: more rare

though

though not lefs worthy of imitation, is the fort of attachment
your Lordfhip has always fhewn
to your corps.

It has been your praife, my Lord,
when out of the field, to forego
the pleafures which high rank,
fortune, youth, and accomplifh-
ments opened to your view, and
to brave the feverity of climate,
through tedious winters, in mere
military fellowfhip.

In retired quarters, you found
the care of your men to be at
once the true preparation for your
country's fervice, and a moft
gratifying enjoyment to your own
benevolence: while on their parts,
they

they confidered their leader as their beft friend and benefactor. Difcipline was thus placed upon a bafis that mechanical valor can never eftablifh, upon a principle worthy of troops who can think and feel, *confidence* and *gratitude*.

Duly impreffed with thefe and many other of your virtues---many more than you would permit me to enumerate; I have the honor to be

My Lord,

Your Lordfhip's moft obedient,

And moft devoted

Humble Servant,

THOMAS ANBUREY.

PREFACE.

THE following letters were written to gratify private friendſhip, and would never have been intruded upon the Public, but from the entreaties of ſome of the moſt reſpeⱪtable Subſcribers to the Work, who flattered the Author, that as they contained much authentic information, relative to America, little known on this ſide of the Atlantic, they could not fail of being intereſting to the Public.

Their

Their ſtyle and manner will clearly
evince them to be the actual reſult of a
familiar correſpondence, and by no means
void of thoſe inaccuracies neceſſarily ariſ-
ing from the rapid effuſions of a confeſ-
fedly inexperienced Writer, which will
ſcarcely be wondered at, by thoſe who
conſider how widely different are the qua-
lifications neceſſary to form the Soldier
and the Author.

Every thing the Reader may meet with
will not appear ſtrictly *nouvelle*; but this
is a circumſtance unavoidably attending
the writer of a tour through a country,
which has been already the ſubject of ſo
much diſcuſſion; but there are certainly
many new circumſtances related, which
will ſerve to point out the true character
and manners of the Americans.

The

The facts came within his own knowledge, or are fupported by fome honour-
able authority; and his motto has ever
been,

> ————Nothing extenuate,
> Nor fet down aught in Malice.

They will ftrike every man with the
greater force, after the evident partiality
of a late Author, who has been led to
reprefent the Favorers of Independence
as poffeffed of every amiable qualification,
and thofe who efpoufed the rights of the
Mother Country, as deftitute of common
feelings, and humanity itfelf.

The Author, fenfible how much thofe
Subfcribers, whofe generofity has exceeded
the limits of the fubfcription, would be
hurt by a particular diftinction, co-
jointly renders them thofe thanks,

> " Which the tried heart that feels alone can give."

DIRECTIONS FOR PLACING THE PLATES.

VOL. I.

VOL. II.

SUBSCRIBERS

T O

THE WORK.

HIS ROYAL HIGHNESS—THE DUKE OF YORK
HIS ROYAL HIGHNESS—PRINCE WILLIAM HENRY
HIS ROYAL HIGHNESS—THE DUKE OF GLOUCESTER
HIS ROYAL HIGHNESS—THE DUKE OF CUMBERLAND

A

His Grace———The Duke of Argyle
The Right Hon.———The Earl of Altamont
The Right Hon.———Lord Audley
The Hon. Lady———Harriet Ackland
His Excellency———Baron D'Alvenſleben

THE ROYAL REGIMENT OF ARTILLERY:

Lieut. Col. Walker
———————Johnſton

SUBSCRIBERS.

Major Williams
———— Lemoine
———— Blomefield
Captain Houghton
————Dyfart
——— ——Willington
——— ——Whitworth
————Collier
————Remington
——— ——Howarth
——— ——Hadden
Lieut. Reed
—— — Neville
———— Sutton
Surgeon Mr. Wild

Major Affleck,————Portland-Street
Capt. Armftrong, (8 Regt. of Foot)
James Abel, Efq.————Cloak-Lane
John Adams, Efq.
Alexander Adair, Efq.————Pall Mall
Mrs. Towers Allen,—Queen's-Square
Mr. A. C. Arnold,————Loweftoff
Mr. Rd. Aldridge,————Briftol
Mr. Wm. Auftin,————Idol-Lane
Ainfley's Library,————Edinburgh
Andrews's Library, ————Worcefter
Mr. Axtell,————Cornhill
James P. Andrews, Efq.
Amicable Society,————Northampton

B

The Rt. Hon.————The Earl of Buckinghamfhire
The Rt. Hon.————The Earl of Barrymore
The Rt. Hon.————The Earl of Balcarres
The Rt. Hon.————The Countefs of Balcarres
The Rt. Hon.————The Earl of Breadalbane
The Rt. Hon.————Vifcount Barrington
The Rt. Hon.————Vifcount Beauchamp
The Rt. Hon.————Lord Brownlow

SUBSCRIBERS.

———— Braddyll, Efq.
Mrs. Braddyll
Sir Robert Barker, Bart.
Sir William Auguftus Brown, Bart.
Richard Benyon, Efq. M. P.
General Burgoyne
Dr. Brocklefby, ——Norfolk-Street
Lieut. Col. Bowyer, (66 Regt.)
Capt. Bell, (19 Regt.)
Lieut. Col. Baillie, ——Edinburgh
Capt. Bowen, Independent Comp.
Capt. Barrette,———— Doncafter, (100 Regt.)
Lieut. Budworth, (72 Regt.)
Richard Barwell, Efq. M. P.
———— Blomfield, Efq.
John Bax, Efq.——Prefton, Kent
John Benjafield, Efq.—— Parliament-Street
Thomas Beardmore, Efq.——Temple
Mr. John Berry,——Canterbury-Square
The Rev. Mr. Bowcher,——Piccadilly
George Biggins, Efq. ——Eflex-Street
Ynyr Burgefs, Efq.——Eaft India Houfe
The Rev. Dr. Bate,——Walton
Lieut. Bartlet, (Royal Engineers)——Chatham
Mr. Broughton,——Treafury
Mr. John Breadhower,——Portfmouth
Mr. Barnikle,——Plymouth
Mr. Burtenfhaw's Library,——Brighthelmftone
Thomas Bowes, Efq.
Mr. Bull's Library, —— Bath
Mr. Thomas Batchelor,——Briftol
Mr. Beazeley,——Black-Friars Road
Mr. J. B. Becket,——Briftol
John Bourchier, Efq.——Ipfwich
Mr. Barrukel
Rob. Barrett, Efq.——London
Capt. Arthur Buttell,——Marines
James Betts, Efq.——Eflex-Street
Wm. Butler, Efq.——Greffe-Street
Mr. Baker's Library,——Southampton
Mr. Barry's Library, ——Haftings

C

The Rt. Hon.——The Earl of Chesterfield
The Rt. Hon.——The Earl of Carlisle
The Rt. Hon.——The Earl of Cholmondeley
The Rt. Hon.——The Earl of Camden
The Rt. Hon.——The Earl of Cavan
The Rt. Hon.——Lord Craven
The Rt. Hon.——Lord Clifford
The Rt. Hon.——Lord Carberry
The Rt. Hon.——Lord Cathcart
The Rt. Hon.——Lord Fred. Campbell
Sir Wm. Clerke, Bart.
Sir Hy. Gough Calthorpe,
Sir Henry Clinton, K. B.
General Christie,——Leicester-Square
Major Campbell, (24 Regt. of Foot)
Capt. Cotter, (103 Regt.)
Bryan Cooke, Esq.
Mrs. Cooke
Wm. Cowden, Esq.——Meuse
Ralph Clayton, Esq.
Richard Crofts, Esq.——Pall Mall
The Rev. Mr. Cove,——Helstone
Mrs. Casement, ——ditto
James Crowdy, Esq.——Swindon, Wilts
Mr. Jos. Colborne, Surgeon,——Brentwood
Mr. Edm. Cotterell,—— Cold Bath Fields
Mr. James Cooper,——Swithin's-Lane
Dr. Cockall
Mr. Thomas Conder,——Aldersgate Street
The Rev. Mr. Crutwell,——Oakingham
James Cobb, Esq.——East India House
Mr. Crawford's Library,——Brighthelmstone
Jos. Chew, Esq Sec. for India Affairs,——North America.
William Curtis, Esq.——London
Lieut. Crichton, (31 Regt.)——Gosport
J. Croft, Esq.

SUBSCRIBERS.

D

His Grace——The Duke of Devonſhire
The Rt. Hon.——The Earl of Derby
The Rt. Hon.——The Earl of Dartmouth
The Rt. Hon.——The Earl of Donegal
The Rt. Hon.——The Counteſs of Darnley
The Rt. Hon.——Viſcount Duncannon
The Rt. Hon.——Viſcount Dalrymple
The Rt. Hon.——Lord Ducie
The Rt. Hon.——Lord Dorcheſter
Colonel Dundas
Lieut. Will. Dalton, (Royal Navy)——Rotherhithe
Lieut. Col. Delancey, Margaret-Street, Cavendiſh-Square
Major Dalrymple, (49 Regt. of Foot)
Capt. Duncan
Richard Dowding, Eſq.——Shadwell
Mr. George Dixon,——Wooburne
Mr. John Dew,——Shenfield
Mr. B. U. Dowſon,——Geldeſton
The Rev. D. Davies,——Macclesfield
Dulot and Owen's Library,——Brighthelmſtone
Meſſ. Downes and March,——Yarmouth
The Rev. H. Bate Dudley, Bradwell
Rich. Jles Dimſdale, Eſq.

E

The Rt. Hon.——The Earl of Effingham
The Rt. Hon.——The Earl of Eglingtoune
The Rt. Hon.——The Earl of Euſton
The Rt. Hon.——Lord Elphinſtone
Sir James Erſkine, Bart.——Cavendiſh-Square

THE ROYAL ENGINEERS.

Major General Sir William Greene, Bart.
Lieut. Col. Moncrief
Capt. Twiſs

SUBSCRIBERS.

Capt. Rudyard
Lieut. Beatfon
——— Courture
——— Bartlett
Mrs. Edgar,———Percy-Street
Mrs. Edwards,———Savage-Gardens
Mr. Thomas Evans,———Minories

F

The Rt. Hon. ———The Earl of Fauconberg
The Rt. Hon.———Vifcount Falmouth
The Rt. Hon.———Vifcount Fielding
The Rt. Hon.———Charles James Fox
The Rt. Hon.———M. Fitzpatrick

FIRST (OR KING'S) REGIMENT OF DRAGOON GUARDS.

General Sir George Howard, K. B.
Lieut. Col. Vyfe
Capt. Trotter
Lieut. Hawley
——— Syer
——— Beckford
——— Serjeantfon
——— Need
Cornet Hamilton

FIRST REGIMENT OF FOOT GUARDS.

Colonel Bertie
——— Strickland
——— *Hon.* Francis Needham
——— *Hon.* H. F. Stanhope
——— Sir Charles Afgill, Bart.

FIFTEENTH REGIMENT OF FOOT.

Lieut. Gen. Sir. Wm. Fawcett
Lieut. Col. Myers

SUBSCRIBERS.

Capt. Madden
—— Ditmas
—— Paumier
—— Spencer
—— Gordon
—— Brown
—— Cockburne
Lieut. Ball
————Stopford
Enſign Barnard
—— Mc Donald
Qr. Maſter Watkins
Surgeon Mr. Anderſon

FORTY-SIXTH REGIMENT OF FOOT.

Lieut. Col. Hon. Colin Lindſay
Major Leighton
Capt. Bell
—— Wale
Lieut. Lloyd
————James
————Dallas

FORTY-SEVENTH REGIMENT OF FOOT.

Lieut. Col. Irving
Major Coote
————Alcock
————Aubrey
Capt. Sir Henry Marr
—— Featherſtone
Lieut. Johnſon
————Hill
————Baldwin
————Mc Lean

FORTY-EIGHTH REGIMENT OF FOOT.

Lieut. Col. Hedges
Major D'Arcy

SUBSCRIBERS.

Major Campbell
Capt. Jones
Lieut. Jones
—— Roberts
Enfign Beevor
—— Power

Colonel Forbes,————Arlington-Street
Lieut. Col. Forfter, (66 Regt. Foot)
Thomas Forfyth, Efq.————New Bond-Street
Cuthbert Fifher, Efq.————Tower
J. Flint, Efq.————Shrewfbury
Mr. Fletcher,————Liverpool 2 fets
Mr. Forreft,————St. Martin's-Lane
Rofe Fuller, Efq.————Wigmore-Street
Walter Farquhar, Efq.————Great Marlborough-Street
Mr. Firmin,————Strand
Thomas Fortune, Efq.————London
Mr. Fenno's Library,————Colchefter

G

His Grace————The Duke of Grafton
His Grace————The Duke of Gordon
The Rt. Hon.————Earl Grofvenor
The Rt. Hon.————Earl of Glafgow
The Rt. Hon.————Lord Gage
General Gordon
Capt. Gwynn
Lieut. Gordon,————Parliament-Street
—— Grant, Efq.
Richard Gray, Efq.————Pall Mall
Mrs. Gibfon,————Hertford-Street
Samuel Greaves, Efq.————Manchefter
The Rev. Mr. Gryll,————Helftone
Mr. T. Gryll,   ditto
Thomas Glynn, Efq.
The Rev. Mr. Gilbert,————Helftone
Mr. Gardner,————London

SUBSCRIBERS.

H

His Grace————The Duke of Hamilton
The Rt. Hon.————The Earl of Huntingdon
The Rt. Hon.————The Earl of Harrington
The Rt. Hon.————The Earl of Harcourt
The Rt. Hon.————The Earl of Hertford
The Rt. Hon.————Lord Howard
The Rt. Hon.————Lord Hawke
The Rt. Hon.————Lord Hawkesbury
The Rt. Hon.————Lord Heathfield
The Rt. Hon.————Lord Hood
The Rt. Hon.————Lord Archibald Hamilton
The Rt. Hon.————Lord Spencer Hamilton
Sir Watts Horton, Bart.
The Hon. Mrs. Horton
The Hon. Lady Horton
The Rev. Mr. Horton
The Hon. Mr. Heneage
Mr. Harman, Princes-Street, oppofite the Manfion-Houfe

THE ROYAL REGIMENT OF HORSE GUARDS.

The Rt. Hon.————General Conway
Col. Balthwayt
Capt. Milnes
———— Chaplin
———— Jefferfon

Col. Harnage,————Parliament-Street
Major Hawker,————ditto
Capt. Hanchett
Capt. Hardy
Major Haines,————Hampfhire
Mr. Hall, Surgeon, (51 Regt.)
The Rev. Mr. Hornby
Mrs. Hindes,————Hertford-Street
John Hawkins, Efq.————Helftone
James Watfon Hull, Efq.————Belvedere, Ireland
b

SUBSCRIBERS,

Trevor Hull, Efq. ———Greek-Street
Mr. Hinckes,———Great Portland-Street
Mr. John Harding,———Strand
Mr. Hollyoake, ——— Red Lion-Square
Mr. Harris,——— St. Mary Axe
Anthony Highmore, Efq. ditto
Edward Heylin, Efq.———Iflington
Mr. Hope,———Upper Seymour-Street, Cavendifh-Square
Benj. Henfhaw, Efq ———Hodfdon
Thomas Hodgfon, Efq ———Briftol
Meff. Haydon and Sons,———Plymouth
The Gentlemens Book Club———at Helftone
Col. Hill, (late of the 9th Regt.)———Helftone
Capt. Richard Hill, ———Helftone
William Hofte, Efq. Barwick
Mr. George Hall,———Star-Office, Exeter-Street

I

The Rt. Hon.———The Earl of Jerfey
Lieut. Col. Jacques, (51 Regt. of Foot)
Sir John Johnfon, Superintendant to the Indians in Canada
Col. Jeffop,———Fludyer-Street
Lieut. Jones,———Lower Brook-Street
Gen. Johnfon
Alex. Irvine, Efq.———Berner's-Street
Mr. Richard Johns,———Helftone
Mr. Johnfon,———Piccadilly
Mr. Samuel Johnfon,———Briftol

K

The Rt Hon.———Lord Kenfington
Lieut. Col. Kingfton, (28 Regt. of Foot)
Capt. Kempthorne,———Helftone
——— Kellett, Efq.———Ruffel-Street, **Covent-Garden**
John Keene, Efq.———Manfion Houfe
Mr. James Kerby,———London
Mr. Charles Knight,———Windfor
Mr. Frederic Kanmacher

SUBSCRIBERS.

L

His Grace———The Duke of Leeds
The Rt. Hon.———The Marquifs of Lanfdown
The Rt. Hon.———The Marquifs of Lothain
The Rt. Hon.———The Earl Ludlow
The Rt. Hon.———Lord Lovaine
The Hon.———Robert Lindfay
The Hon.———Capt. John Lindfay
The Hon———Hugh Lindfay
Sir Michael Le Fleming, Bart.———Hertford-Street
General Lambton,———Harley-Street
Paul Le Mefurier, Efq.—M.P.—Walbrook
Charter Layton, Efq.———Drayton
Mr. Loxley,———Poultry
Mr. Lofack,———Wigmore-Street
Mr. John Lee,———Black-Friars
Mr. Leigh,———Thorndon
Mr. John Lees,———Brentford

M

His Grace———The Duke of Marlborough
His Grace———The Duke of Montrofe
The Rt. Hon.———Vifcount Mount Edgecumbe
The Rt. Hon.———Vifcount Molefworth.
The Rt. Hon.———Vifcount Melbourne
The Rt. Hon.———Vifcount Mountftuart
The Rt. Hon.———Lord Milford
Richard Mafter, Efq. M P —Charles-Street, BerkleyqSq.
J. Madocks, Efq. (Coldftream Regt. Gds.) Bedford-ftreet
Major Money,———Norwich
Capt. Mc. Kinnon,———(63 Regt.) Ireland
Capt. Robert Mc. Crea,———Guernfey
Cuthbert Mafhiter, Efq.———Romford
Edward Mafon, Efq.———Spital-Fields
The Rev. Mr. Mingin,———Golden-Square
Mr. Mackreth,———Scotland-Yard
Mr. Jofeph Mitchell,———Helftone
J. Milbanke, Efq.

SUBSCRIBERS.

The Rev. Dr. Morgan,——St. James's-Square
James Madden, Efq.——St. Albans-Street
Thomas Maude, Efq.——Temple
Mr. Mc Leifh's Library, Edinburgh

N

His Grace——The Duke of Northumberland

THE NINTH REGIMENT OF FOOT.

Lieut. Col. Campbell
Major Ritchie
Capt. Baillie
—— Hoey
—— Buchannan
—— Spencer
—— Vincent
—— Timms
—— Murray
—— Piercy
—— Rofe
—— Mc Lean
Lieut. Reynolds
——Mitchell
—— Fatio
Enfigns James Rofe
—— Duffe
—— Dalziel
—— Burbridge
—— O'Connor
Enfign Keightley
—— Wolfe
Chaplain—The Rev. Mr. Clewlow

THE ROYAL NAVY.

Admiral Montague
Capt. Dacres

SUBSCRIBERS.

—— Hardy
—— Schanks
Lieut. Wm. Dalton
—— Wm. Bentick
Mrs. Newberry,——St. Paul's Church-Yard

O

Sir George Ofborn, Bart. Charles-Street, Berkley-Square
James Ormfby, Efq.——Dublin

P

His Grace——The Duke of Portland
Her Grace——The Dutchefs of Portland
The Rt. Hon.——The Earl of Plymouth
The Rt Hon.——The Earl of Powis
The Rt. Hon.——Vifcount Palmerftone
The Rt, Hon.——Lord Pelham
The Rt. Hon.——Lord Petre
The Hon.——Mr. Petre, Grofvenor-Square
The Hon.——Mr. G. Petre, Somerfet-Street
The Hon.——Thomas Pelham, Stretton-Street
The Hon.——General Parker
Gen. Pitt,——Tenterden-Street
Capt. Peacock,——(17 Regt. of Foot)
Mr. Pugh,——Poultry
Mrs. Piozzi,——Hanover-Square
Mr. Phillips, Somerfetfhire
Mr. Thomas Powell,——Terace, Buckingham-Street
Mr. Parnell,——Church-Street, Spital-Fields
Capt. Walter Proffer,——Ireland
Palmer and Merrick's Library,——Oxford
Mr. Powell,——Newgate-Street
Punchard and Jermyns's Library, Ipfwich
Thomas Boothby Parkyns, Efq.
Thomas Paulk, Efq.

SUBSCRIBERS.

R

The Rt. Hon.————The Earl of Radnor
The Rt. Hon.———— Lord Rivers
The Rt. Hon.————Lord Rodney
The Rt. Hon.————Lord Rawdon
Sir Matthew White Ridley, Bart.————Portland-Place
Capt. Reed,————(103 Regt.)
Mr. Robson,———— Princes-Street, Hanover-Square
Mr. Alexander Roberts,————Red Lion-Square
John Rogers, Esq ————Helstone
E. Read, Esq. Chester
George Rome, Esq. Mount-Street
John Le Chevalier Roome, Esq.————London-Road
Mr. Rush,————Fountain-Street
Alexander Raby, Esq.————Cobham
Mrs. Raby
Mr. Robinson,————Cornhill

S

His Grace————The Duke of St. Albans
The Rt. Hon.————The Earl of Suffolk
The Rt. Hon.————The Earl of Shaftesbury
The Rt. Hon.————The Countess Dow. of Shaftesbury
The Rt. Hon.————The Earl of Scarborough
The Rt. Hon.————The Earl of Stanhope
The Rt. Hon.————Earl Spencer
The Rt. Hon.————The Earl Stamford
The Rt. Hon.————Viscount Stormont
The Rt. Hon.————Lord Say and Sele
The Rt. Hon.————Lord Stourton
The Rt. Hon.————Lord St. John
The Rt. Hon.————Lord Scarsdale
The Rt. Hon.————Lord Southampton
The Rt. Hon.————Lord Robert Spencer
The Rt. Hon ————Lady Ann Simpson
The Hon.———— Mr. Sandilands
Thomas Stanley, Esq. M. P.————Pall Mall
R. B. Sheridan, Esq. M.P.———— Bruton Street

SUBSCRIBERS.

SECOND (OR ROYAL N. BRITISH) REGT. OF DRAGOONS.

Major Ramfay
Capt. Seaford
—— Smith
—— Boardman
Lieut. Fortefcue
Cornet Wigley
—— Bothwell
—— Leigh

SIXTEENTH (OR QUEEN'S) REGT. OF LIGHT DRAGOONS.

The Hon. ——Major General Harcourt
Major Gardner
——*Hon*. H. Bennett
—— Howell
Capt. Boyce
—— Carmichael
Lieut. Hawker
——Smallett
——Archer
——Munro
Cornet Afhton
——Lee
——Pennyman
Cornet Anfon
——Deering

SIXTY-SECOND REGIMENT OF FOOT.

Major Gen.——Matthews
Lieut. Col. —— Campbell
Major Howe
Capt. Banbury
—— Sotheron
—— Wybrants
—— Blackall

SUBSCRIBERS,

—— Matthias
—— Bromhead
—— Blacker
—— Vallancey
Lieut. James
—— Brudenell
—— Gourlay
—— Batchelor
—— Kerr
Enſign Kent
—— Garden

Major Skene,——Chelſea
Lieut. Stuart
Mr. Seddon,——Alderſgate-Street
John Sawrey, Eſq.—— Lancaſhire
Edw. Spike, Eſq.
Mrs. Spike
Miſs Spike
Mr. John Slade,—— Camberwell
Daniel Seton, Eſq.——Stratford-Place
Mr. Shiercliffe,——Briſtol
Mr. Charles Spitta,——College-Hill
John Scott, Eſq.——Wigmore-Street
Capt. Scott, ——(53 Regt of Foot)
Mr. Scott, Jun.——Norwich
Miſs Smiths,——Percy-Street
James Simmonds, Eſq. Banker, ——Canterbury
Simmons and Kirby, Canterbury
John Seleer, Eſq.——London
Mr. Stalker,——London
Mr. Sollors,——Blandford
The Rev. Mr. Salmon
Mr. J. F. Souel,——Guernſey
John Secker, Eſq.——Windſor
Stell's Library,——Haſtings

SUBSCRIBERS.

T

The Rt. Hon. ———The Marquiſs of Titchfield
The Rt. Hon.———Lord Torphichen
The Hon. ———Mr. Twiſleton Thompſon
Sir Charles Thompſon, Bart. K.B. Bond-Street
Sir John Thorold, Bart. ———Cavendiſh-Square

THE THIRD REGIMENT OF HORSE, OR CARBINEERS.

Colonel Longfield
Major Wilford
———Willey
Capt. Smith
——— Tiſdale
——— Roſs
Lieut. Daniel
———French
———Templeton
———Fitzgerald
———Sir Thomas Chapman
Cornet Cramer
———Gilleſpie
———Longfield
———*Hon.* Geo. Pomroy
———Duncombe
Surgeon James Wallace

THE THIRD (OR PRINCE OF WALES's) REGT. OF DRAG. GUARDS.

Major Gen. Phillipſon
Col. Manſell
Capt. Milbanke
——— Charlton
Lieut. Charlton
Cornet Dotten

TWENTIETH REGIMENT OF FOOT.

Colonel Lind
Major Hon. S. D. Strangeways
———Rollinſon

SUBSCRIBERS.

Capt. Winchester
—— Norman
Lieut. Bateman
———Brooke
Ensign Wynyard

TWENTY-FIRST REGT. OF FOOT (OR R N B) FUZILEERS.

Colonel Hamilton
Major Lovell
Capt. Petrie
—— Brodie
Lieut. Grant
———Dalgleish
————Congalton
Qr. M. Geo. Lauder

TWENTY-FOURTH REGIMENT OF FOOT.

Lieut. Gen. Wm. Tayler
Lieut. Col. England
Major Pilmer
———Campbell
Capt. Blake
—— Stiel
—— W. Doyle
Lieut. Leybourne
———Short
————Hollings
Ensign Meyrick

General Trapaud, ——-Berner's-Street
Col. Anstruther Thompson,—(late of 62 Regt.) Edinburgh
Samuel Toulmin, Esq.———Walbrook
Mr. James Turner, Jun.———Milbank
Thomas Trewin, Esq.——Helstone
John Trevener, Esq.——ditto
Mr. William Terwin,——Haymarket
Mr. Templeman,——Size-Lane
Edward Thornycroft, Esq.——Chester
Mr. William Trufton,——Brentwood
Mr. John Thomas
Rev. Mr. Hen. Hawkins Tremayne, A.M. Heligan, Cornwall
Mr. Leigh Thorndon,
Thomas Fortune, Esq.——London

SUBSCRIBERS.

Mr. Thurgood,——Fenchurch Street
David Thomas, Esq.——Pay Master in America

U

The Rt. Hon.——The Earl of Upper Offory
Mr. Benjamin Uphill,——Mount-Street, Grosvenor-Square
Cornelius Vanderftop, Esq.——Princes-St. Hanover-Sq.

W

The Rt. Hon.——The Earl of Weftmoreland
The Rt. Hon.——The Earl of Winchelfea
The Rt. Hon.——The Earl of Waldegrave
The Rt. Hon.——The Earl of Warwick
The Rt. Hon.——Vifcount Weymouth
The Rt. Hon.——Lord Willoughby de Broke
The Rt. Hon.——Lord Walpole
Sir Watkin Williams Wynne, Bart.——St. James's-Square
Sir George Warren, K B.——Grafton-Street
Mifs Warburton
General Warde
Capt. Willoe,——(8 Regt. of Foot)
—— Wifeman,——(53 Regt. of Foot)
Edward Wilford, Esq.——Chelfea
—— Williamfon, Esq.——Temple
Richard Whatley, Esq.——Parliament-Street
Rev. Mr. Whatley,————ditto
Rev. Mr. Wills,——Helftone
Mr. John Whitehead,——Bafinghall-Street
Mr. Thomas Wagftaff,——Highgate
Mr. John Winpenny,——Briftol
Robert Woodriff, Esq.——Temple
Mr. Matthew White,——St. Swithin's-Lane
Woodmafon and Page,——Leadenhall-Street
James Woodmafon, Esq.——Bond-Street

Y

Major William Young

ERRATA.

T R A V E L S

THROUGH THE

INTERIOR PARTS

OF

A M E R I C A,

L E T T E R   I.

Cork, August 8th, 1776.

MY DEAR FRIEND,

I RECEIVED your letter, dated the 2d
inftant, and furely nothing can be
more flattering than the warm teftimony
of regard and friendfhip every line of it
fpeaks.—It was with great reluctance you
confented to my going into the army, but
a dull inactive life neither fuited my circumftances nor my inclination, and an early

VOL. I.   B   love

love of a military one, foon determined
my choice.   My time and poor abilities
cannot be fo well employed, as in the fervice of my King and country.

I have no regrets at quitting England,
but the lofs I muft fuftain in your pleafant
and improving converfation; and am perfuaded you will alleviate as many of thofe
painful reflections as poffible, by taking
every opportunity of writing to me.—
None fhall be omitted, on my part, of
affuring you how often I think of you,
and the implicit attention I fhall ever pay
to your commands, in giving you a defcription of perfons, places, and various
occurrences—and fhould I fometimes be
too particular on trivial fubjects, you muft
excufe it, and remember the two prevailing
motives you affigned for this kind of cor-
refpondence—the pleafure you was fo obliging to fay it would afford you, and the
utility you thought it would be of to me,

by

by calling my attention to whatever became in the leaft worthy of obfervation.

This is the laft you muft expect from me on this fide the Atlantic, as in a few days we fail, with the care of fome recruits for the 47th regiment.

I once more entreat you, my dear friend, to take every opportunity of writing to me, and believe that time and diftance can never abate the refpect and friendfhip with which I am,

Yours, &c.

LET-

L E T T E R   II.

On board the Howe, on the } Sept. 11th,
Banks of Newfoundland. }   1776.

MY DEAR FRIEND,

IT would be very ungrateful indeed not to embrace the opportunity, by a ſhip that is bound for England, now lying too for letters, to ſend you a haſty account of the events that have happened ſince my departure from Ireland.

You know I had the care of ſome recruits for the 47th regiment; and as they were compoſed of that nation, no leſs famous for their characteriſtic errors, than their ſpirit and unbounded hoſpitality, let me relate a caſual occurrence or two, in place of novelty, which cannot be expected, ed, fituated as I am, between fky and water.

There were continually fome little difputes among thefe Hibernians. One day, on hearing a more than ufual noife upon deck, I went up to enquire the occafion of it, and learnt it was a quarrel between two of them. Upon afking the caufe of him who appeared the tranfgreffor, he exclaimed, " Oh! and plaife your Honor, I " did nothing to him at all, at all"---when the other haftily replied, " Oh yes, and " plaife your Honor, he faid as how he " would take up a ftick and blow my " brains out." The peculiar manner in which it was vociferated, was fo truly comic, that I could not refrain from laughter, and merely reprimanding them, overlooked the offence.

The weather has been very pleafant, 'till a few days previous to our coming on

thefe

thefe Banks, when there enfued a moft
dreadful ftorm. The fhip was unable to
carry the leaft fail, being left to the fury
of the driving tempeft, it was impoffible
for any one to keep the deck, and the helm
was lafhed hard of weather.

About the third day the ftorm began to
abate, and the evening became almoft
calm. But there was fuch a prodigious
fwell of the fea, that the fhip was expected every moment to roll her mafts overboard: fhe had driven fo much to the lee-
ward, that although we could not difcern
land, the yards and rigging were covered
with birds, that were blown from it by the
ftorm.

At this time, one of my recruits coming upon deck, not obferving any one
there, and the fea fo tremendous, immediately went below, and cried out to his
companions, " Oh ! by my foul, honeys, the
" fea

" fea is very dreadful, and we are all fure
" to be drowned, for the fhip's a finking.
" However, I have this confolation, that
" if fhe goes to the bottom, the Captain
" muft be accountable for us when we get
" to Quebec." And his fears operated fo
powerfully, that he gave a groan, and
fainted away.

A few days after this the fea, which
before had been fo tremendous, and to ufe
the technical phrafe, run mountains high,
was now become as calm as a mill-pond.
It is cuftomary, on fuch weather, in a
fleet, for one fhip to invite the Captains
and paffengers of others to dinner. The
mode of invitation on thefe occafions, is
by hoifting a table-cloth to the enfign-
ftaff.

We hung out this fignal, and the Captain of the neareft fhip, with an officer,
came on board. After dinner, fo fudden

B 4   and

and ftrong a breeze fprung up, as to render their return very unfafe, and it was
two days before they could venture, when
even then they accomplifhed it with imminent danger.

This is a little anecdote I cannot help
wifhing to be much noticed, as it might be
a caution to young officers and captains of
fhips, how they make nautical vifits, or
upon any occafion quit their veffels.

Thefe Banks may be ranked amongft the
many furprifing and wonderful works of
nature, being a mountain formed under
water, by the flime that is continually
wafhing away from the Continent.   Its
extent has never yet been afcertained, but
is generally reckoned to be about 160
leagues long, and 90 broad.   About the
middle of it is a kind of bay, called the
Ditch.   The depth of water varies confiderably,

derably, being in fome places only five, and in others fixty fathom. The fun is fcarcely ever to be difcerned, a cold thick fog generally covering the whole atmof-phere, which renders it extremely dan-gerous to a fleet; for it is at times a ftate of total darknefs, where a continual firing of guns, or inceffant noife of the drum, can alone prevent the fhips running foul of each other.

The winds around thefe Banks are ge-nerally very impetuous; the conftant agi-tation of the waves, I am informed, is occa-fioned from the fea being driven by irre-gular currents, that beat fometimes on one fide and fometimes on the other, ftrik-ing with great force againft the borders of thefe Banks, which are every where almoft perpendicular, and repel them with equal violence: and yet, on the Banks themfelves, a little from the coaft, it is as quiet as in a bay,

bay, except there happens to be a ftrong and forced wind coming from a great diftance.

When we found we were upon thefe Banks, which is perceptible without founding, as the water changes from an azure blue to a white fandy color, we laid too in order to fifh for cod, the procefs of which is no lefs entertaining than furprizing to Europeans.

After baiting the hooks with the entrails of a fowl, in a few minutes we caught a fifh, when the failors made ufe of fome part of the entrails, as being a better bait, and then drew up the cod as faft as you can poffibly imagine; for though we remained there only half an hour, we caught as many as would ferve the fhip's crew the reft of the voyage.

You may wonder by what means they are certain of having caught a fifh, with

fo

fo many fathom of line out.   When it has been a little while in the water, they gently pull it with the finger and thumb, and if there is a fifh, the ftruggling of it occafions a vibration of the line, which is very perceptible, though fo many fathoms deep.   They then haul it in, and as foon as the fifh comes in view, the water mag-nifies it to fuch a fize, that it appears almoft impoffible to get it on board; and indeed it requires fome dexterity, for on hauling them out of the water they ftruggle with fuch violence, as frequently to work themfelves off the hooks, by entangling the line in the rigging, before they can be got up the fhip's fide.

But thofe veffels which particularly follow this bufinefs, avoid the inconvenience by erecting galleries on the outfide, from the main-maft to the ftern, and fometimes the whole length of the fhip, in which are placed barrels with the tops ftruck out,

and

and the fifhermen get into thefe to fhelter themfelves from the weather.   Their ftay, I imagine, cannot be long, as the method of curing is equally as expeditious as the catching them; for as foon as the cod is caught, they cut out its tongue, and give it to one who immediately ftrikes off its head, plucks out its liver and entrails, and giving it to another, the bone is drawn out as far as the navel; it is then thrown into the hold of the fhip, where it is falted and ranged in piles.   The perfon who falts it is careful to leave fufficient falt between the rows of fifh, to prevent them touching each other, and yet not too much, as either excefs would fpoil the cod.

The right of fifhing upon the Great Bank, by the law of nature, ought to have been common to all mankind; but England and France, being the only two powers that had colonies in North America, made no fcruple to appropriate to themfelves, what

what Spain certainly had the greateft claim to, as the original difcoverers of it; and who, from the number of her monks and priefts, as well as her religion, might have pleaded the neceffity of keeping. Yet at the conclufion of the laft peace, they entirely gave up all pretenfions to it: fince which time England and France are the only nations that frequent thofe latitudes, and both have frigates continually cruizing, to prevent the encroachments of other nations.

The produce of this fifhery is certainly a moft inexhauftible wealth to both countries, and it is no wonder they are fo very tenacious of it: yet it is furprizing what a large circuit the fhips are obliged to take before their voyage is compleated, and the profits refulting from this fifhery returns to either, nearly traverfing by water half the globe: for, in the firft inftance, they fail from their refpective ports

in

in Europe to thefe Banks, from whence they proceed with their cargoes to the Mediterranean and African iflands, where they difpofe of their fifh for the produce of thofe iflands, then go to the Weft Indies, to exchange that cargo, and return home laden with fugars and rum.

It appears a very fingular circumftance, that thefe Banks fhould abound with cod and no other fifh; and that the greateft philofophers have never been able to account for it.

The Captain of the fhip that is waiting for our letters growing impatient, obliges me to make a hafty conclufion, with wifhing you health and happinefs, and affuring you that you fhall hear from me as foon as I arrive at Quebec.

I am,

Yours, &c.

L E T-

L E T T E R III.

Quebec, Oct. 8th, 1776.

DEAR SIR,

AFTER a fatiguing paſſage of eleven weeks, attended with no little danger, we are ſafe arrived at Quebec, which before I proceed to give you any deſcription of, it will be more methodical to relate the occurrences that befel us the remainder of our voyage.

I told you in my laſt, that we had frigates cruizing on the Banks, one of which informed us, that there were ſeveral privateers in the river Saint Laurence. Had we been leſs attentive to, and more apprehenſive of the ſhoals and ſands that river abounds with, rendering its navigation difficult

ficult and dangerous, it would have been better for us; for a few days after we had paſſed Cape Roſier, a favorable wind ſpringing up, the Captain crouded all the ſail he poſſibly could, in order to get the next morning to the iſle of Bec, where he might find a pilot, being very uneaſy, as he had never been up that river before.

But to our great ſurprize and aſtoniſhment, about one o'clock in the morning, we run right upon a ſhoal (which is called Mille Vache) with amazing violence.

A ſhip belonging to the fleet that had gone a head in the day time, and perceived the ſhoal, (being low water) had immediately brought too, to warn us of our danger, which they did, by firing ſignal guns. But the Captain miſtaking them for thoſe of a privateer, returned the ſhot.

The

'The ſhip beat with great violence, and was every moment expected to go to pieces; but the tide ſoon turning, ſhe reſted upon the ground, and to our great aſtoniſhment, at the break of day, we found ourſelves ſo near the ſhore, that, to uſe a ſea phraſe, we could almoſt chuck a biſcuit on it.

Upon the clearing up of a fog, a ſhip was diſcerned, which proved to be the ſame that had fired guns in the night time: ſhe was then about three leagues diſtant. We immediately fired guns of diſtreſs, of which ſhe took no notice, and imagined ſhe had, as too frequently is the caſe, deſerted us, becauſe we were in diſtreſs and ſtood in need of her aſſiſtance.

However, we found friends in a quarter we little expected, for a canoe with three men paddled from the ſhore, one of whom came on board and told us, we were very fortunate to have ſtruck at the time of

VOL. I.   C   ſpring-

spring-tides, or there would be no probability of the ship's being got off. He directed us, when the tide was coming in, to carry out the bow anchor the length of the cable, and then made no doubt, but at the full, the ship would float again, and we might warp off.

After having given every proper instruction, he took his leave, requesting, at the same time, that in case we were so unfortunate as not to effect it, we would come ashore to his house, offering every assistance to save the cargo, and with a sloop of his to take us up the river.

At the return of the tide some men were sent out with the anchor, according to the directions given; at the heighth of it we floated, and to the joyful satisfaction of every one, got clear off, sustaining no other damage than the loss of two anchors: yet such was the Captain's care and anxiety for

his

his owners, that, I am perfuaded, he would not have expreffed half the concern for the lofs of the whole fhip's burthen and company, that he did for his anchors: as with Captains of hired tranfports, the crew and the cargo are but fecondary objects.

This is one inftance of the numberlefs accidents that await tranfports, by which, I am convinced, the fervice is retarded, and many operations, however critical, which depend on troops and provifion, are often fruftrated, either by defign or negligence. For only figure to yourfelf what a fituation an army of fo many thoufands as that we have upon the Continent, and thofe chiefly fed with provifions from the Mother Country, muft be in, upon the flighteft delay.

It is much to be lamented, therefore, that all tranfports are not commanded by King's officers, or at leaft the mafter made

more

more fubject to controul, when under
convoy, or naval orders; as it would
prevent the inconvenience and hazard that
is continually happening to the King's
fervice.

You will fuppofe it furprizing that this
has never been noticed and remedied by
thofe in power. I fhould have thought
the affair of the powder-fhip that went
into Bofton, would have occafioned a
thorough inveftigation of this iniquitous
bufinefs.

The Captains of tranfports in general,
are a fet of people who have their own intereft much more at heart than the welfare
of their country; and it is well known
that many of them are difaffected to Government, which was the cafe of the Captain of the fhip juft alluded to, but where
the blame is to be imputed, is not for me
to fay. As in all probability you may
not

not have heard of this affair, or the real truth of it may not have reached you, I shall relate the matter, as I had it from a Captain of a fhip who failed in the fame fleet, whofe veracity can be relied on, and from the amazing ftrange circumftances which attended the lofs of that fhip, you may form your own opinions.

It feems this veffel was an immenfe charge, containing 1500 barrels of gunpowder, befides a great quantity of other warlike ftores. · Several perfons well difpofed to Government, and who were perfectly aquainted with the Captain's principles, informed thofe who had the direction of tranfports at Cork, that this man would, the very firft opportunity, leave the convoy and join the Americans, but no attention was paid to the information; upon which they expreffed their apprehenfions to the Captain of the frigate was to convoy them out, who promifed to

C 3   take

take all poſſible care of that ſhip during the voyage: and every one in the fleet thought he was not the man repreſented, as he kept cloſe under the ſtern of the frigate.

When the fleet came off Boſton harbour, a frigate that was cruizing for the purpoſe, informed them, that the King's troops had evacuated Boſton, and gone to Halifax; and in the fleet's ſailing to that place, in one of thoſe fogs that I have already deſcribed to you, the Captain of the powder-ſhip ſeized the opportunity, left the fleet, and ſailed back for Boſton, at the mouth of which harbour was ſtationed a fifty-gun ſhip, to prevent any veſſel from going in, that might have eſcaped any of the frigates that were cruizing.

Upon the Captain of the tranſport's being interrogated by the man of war, he acknowledged himſelf bound for Boſton,

ton, that he had not heard of the troops evacuating it, and feveral more excufes; but fome doubts and fufpicions arifing from the man's converfation, and fhe being found a fhip of fuch an immenfe treafure, an officer was fent on board her, and as the evening was coming on, lafhed her to his main-maft, intending to fail her the next morning for Halifax, under the beft convoy he could afford.

But to fhew you what a determined villain the Captain of the tranfport was, in the night time, he confined the Lieutenant, who was fent on board, cut away from the man of war, and under cover of the night, made all poffible expedition to get into Bofton

The tide would not anfwer his purpofe that time, and the man of war could not come up to her, for want of a fufficient

C 4   depth

depth of water. The Captain manned his pinnace, and fent another Lieutenant on board her. Upon the officer's attempting it, the Captain ftruck a harpoon into his fkull; he fell into the boat, and the reft finding a great refiftance, and that they were likely to be overpowered, rowed back again.

The tide now turned, and he got the fhip fafe under the cannon of the Americans, before a greater force could be difpatched to retake poffeffion of her.

The lofs on our fide was great indeed, but the advantage to the Americans was tenfold, as they were in the utmoft diftrefs for thofe materials, and which event may in fome meafure procraftinate this unfortunate war.

Two days after our late accident, we arrived off the ifle of Condre, where we got a pilot, a pilot, and three days after anchored fafe in the bafon of this city.

Fearful of being too late to fend this by a fhip that is juft failing for England, there is only time to affure you, that I fhall embrace every opportunity of convincing you, with how much fincerity and friend-fhip I am,

Yours, &c.

L E T T E R   IV.

Quebec, October 15th, 1776.

MY DEAR FRIEND,

BEFORE you have any account of this city and its environs, I shall describe to you the river Saint Laurence, which, upon their first sailing up it, is the astonishment and admiration of every European. In forming an idea of a river, people in general are apt to judge by comparison : those who have made the tour of Europe, instantly call to mind the Rhine and the Danube; those who have not, the Thames. What will you say, when you are informed that these, though very noble and beautiful, are but mere rivulets, when

put

put in competition with that of Saint
Laurence.

This river iffues from lake Ontario,
taking its courfe north-eaft, wafhing Montreal, where it receives the Outtuais, forming many fertile iflands, and a lake which
is called St. Pierre.   It continues the fame
courfe, and meets the tide 400 miles from
the fea, where it is navigable for large
veffels.   After receiving in its progrefs in-
numerable ftreams, this great river falls
into the ocean at Cape Rofier; it is there
90 miles broad, where the cold in general is fevere, and the fea rather boifterous.   In its progrefs it forms variety of
bays, harbours and iflands, many of the
latter being extremely fruitful and pleafant.

The river Saint Laurence has ever been
looked upon as a good defence to this province, for in the neighbourhood of Quebec,

it

it abounds with hidden rocks, with ſtrong currents in many places, which force the ſhips to make various windings. From the time that Quebec was beſieged by Sir William Phipps, in the year 1690, who was obliged to retire with a great loſs of ſhipping, this river was very little known to the Engliſh till the year 1759, when Sir Charles Saunders, with a fleet of 50 Engliſh men of war, and near 300 ſail of tranſports, arrived off Quebec, without the loſs of a ſingle ſhip, which clearly proves thoſe dangers were not ſo great as had been repreſented. Since that time it has been better known ; and though we have nót at preſent at this place ſo many men of war, yet there are near as many tranſports, notwithſtanding the navigation up this river from the ſea is rendered very dangerous, by the ſtrength of the current and the number of ſand-banks, which fre-quently ariſe in places where they never appeared before; the fatal conſequences of which

which feveral veffels have experienced this
war,

There are abundance of porpoifes in the
river St. Laurence, which are moftly white,
and when they rife to the furface of the
water, have the appearance of an hog
fwimming. At night, if I may be allowed
the expreffion, without being accufed of
an Iricifm, they caufe moft beautiful *fire*
works in the water: for being in fuch abundance, and darting with amazing velocity,
a continued ftream of light glides through
the water, and as fhoals of them frequently
crofs each other, the luminous appearance
is fo picturefque, that no defcription can
reach it.

On our entering the river St. Laurence,
we faw, off the ifland of Anticofti, a great
number of feals, one of which we caught.
This animal is generally ranked amongft
the clafs of fifh, although produced on
land,

land, and living more there than in water. Its head refembles that of a maftiff, it has four paws which are very fhort, efpecially the hinder ones, ferving rather to crawl, than to walk upon, and refembling fins; but the fore feet have claws; the fkin is exceeding hard and covered with fhort hair; they are firft white, but as they grow up turn to fandy or black, and fome of them are of three different colours.

There are two forts, the larger weighing near two thoufand pounds, and have a fharper fnout than the others. I have been told that the Indians have the art of taming thefe creatures, fo as to make them follow like a dog.

I am led to imagine they couple and bring forth their young on the rocks, from this reafon, wherein the powerful inftinct of nature fhewed itfelf very predominant-ly: one day, feveral large ones that had got

their

their young on their backs, dropt them
now and then into the water and took
them up again, which no doubt, as being
brought forth upon land, was to teach
them to fwim; it is not very furprizing,
when it is confidered this animal is amphibious: but the mode is exactly the fame,
only changing the element, with that of
the feathered creation, whofe little ones
flutter from fpray to fpray, before they
venture to fly abroad. The eagle carries
her young, to train them up to encounter
boifterous winds.

Thefe animals are caught on the coaft of
Labrador. The Canadians go to this frozen
and almoft uninhabitable coaft, in the
middle of October, and remain there till
June; their mode of catching them is by
placing nets between the continent and a
few fmall iflands, where coming in fhoals
from the eaft, in attempting to pafs thefe
ftraights, they are caught; they then convey

vey them to land, where they remain frozen till the month of May; the oil is then extracted from them, and it is said that ·seven or eight of thefe animals will yield a hogfhead. The ufe of its fkin is fo generally known, it needs no defcription; its flefh is allowed to be very good, but if you had partaken of it, as I have done, you would coincide with me in opinion, that it turns to better account when converted into blubber.

The tide goes a league beyond Trois Rivieres, which is thirty leagues higher up the river. The difference of the tide at this place is generally between forty-five and forty-eight feet, but at the new and full moon, from fifty-four to fifty-feven, which is very confiderable.

The river is three quarters of a mile broad here, and as the fea water, though it does not come up immediately to the town,

town, renders it fomewhat brackifh, the inhabitants make ufe of it only for culinary purpofes, having fpring water for their beverage.

In failing up the river St. Laurence, the firft plantations you meet with are about fifty leagues on the fouth, and twenty on the north fide of the river, below Quebec: they are but thinly fcattered, and their produce very indifferent. The fertile fields commence near the capital, which I am informed grow better, the nearer you advance to Montreal.

About half way up the river, we came to the *Ifles aux Oifeaux*, and paffed them about the diftance of a cannon fhot; they are two rocks that rife up in a conical form, about 60 feet above the furface of the water, the largeft of which appeared to be about two or three hundred feet in circumference; they are very near one another,

VOL. I. D and

and there does not appear a fufficient
depth of water between them for a fmall
fhallop. It is difficult to fay what color
thefe are of, as both furface and banks are
entirely covered with the dung of the
birds that refort thither; however, there
were difcernable in places fome veins of a
reddifh caft.

One of the mates of the fhip faid he had
been on them, and had loaded a fmall fhallop with eggs, which were of different
forts, and that the ftench arifing from the
dung was almoft infupportable. Befides
the fea-gulls, and other fowls from the
neighbouring lands, there is found a
fpecies that cannot fly. It appears to me
wonderful, in fo prodigious a multi-
tude of nefts, how every one finds its
own. At my requeft, the Captain of the
fhip fired a cannon fhot, which fpread the
alarm over all this feathered common-
wealth, when there arofe over the two
iflands

iflands a thick cloud of fowl, at leaft two
or three leagues in circuit.

One material circumftance I forgot to
mention to you, happened in our voyage
to this place. In the middle of Auguft,
after we had been incommoded for feveral
days with exceffive heats, one morning,
foon after we got up, we felt fuch an intenfe cold, that both the Captain and myfelf were obliged to put on our great coats.
We could by no means imagine the caufe of
this alteration, the weather being extremely
fine, and particularly as the wind did not
blow from the north. But on the third
morning, juft before day-break, a failor
called out with all his might, " luff, luff,"
which the man at the helm had fcarcely
done, when an enormous piece of ice paffed
along-fide of the veffel, which infallibly
muft have dafhed her to pieces, had fhe
ftruck againft it. At day-break we faw it,
when it appeared to be about fix times as

D 2   large

large as our fhip, and twice the heighth of its mafts. You well know that only one third of ice, while fwimming, appears above water, and when that is confidered, I do not wonder that the ignorant fhould not readily affent to the relations given by travellers, of thefe frozen productions of nature.

Having already fwelled this letter beyond its intended limits, and wifhing to avoid, as much as poffible, being too diffufe on trivial fubjects, I fhall conclude it with my beft wifhes for your welfare and happinefs, affuring you that I am, with friendfhip and efteem,

Yours, &c.

LET-

L E T T E R   V.

Quebec, Oct. 24th, 1776.

DEAR SIR,

AGREEABLE to my promise in a former letter, I shall now proceed in the description of the river St. Laurence, with some occurrences which befel us, previous to our arrival at Quebec.

One of the finest bays to be met with in going up the river, is that of St. Paul, and as we were under the necessity of anchoring opposite to it, till the return of tide, I prevailed on the Captain to go on shore.

D 3   Upon

Upon our landing, the Prieſt of the pariſh came and invited us to his houſe, treating us with much hoſpitality. He was a man rather advanced in years, a native of France, and poſſeſſed of great learning; he had been recommended by the French Court to the Biſhop of Quebec, while this province was under their government, and, as I am afraid is the caſe with too many well deſerving characters, was poorly rewarded, by being made Prieſt of this ſmall pariſh, for ſome eſſential ſervices he had rendered the French, which, however, has many privileges annexed to it.

From the great veneration and reſpect that was ſhewn him, one would naturally conclude he was much beloved by his pariſhioners, and his converſation turned upon making them happy, by inſtructing them both in religious and moral duties, encouraging induſtry, and diveſting them

of

of thofe innate favage difpofitions, which, he obferved, the lower fort of Canadians are but too prone to.

It was impoffible to fay which fhould be moft admired, his fmile of welcome, the neatnefs of the repaft, or the hilarity of his converfation; all of which gave me the greater pleafure, when put in contraft with the other French Priefts I have met with, who are auftere and contracted, and fo difgufting, that rather than fit down with them, I would eat hay with my horfe.

This bay is about eighteen leagues be-low Quebec, containing only this fmall parifh, which is fome diftance from the fhore of the bay, on a low plain, formed by the river. It is furrounded with ex-ceeding high mountains on every fide, ex-cepting one large gap, which runs parallel to the river. The farms are at fome dif-tance from each other, and the church is

D 4　　　　　reckoned

reckoned one of the moft ancient in Canada, which feems confirmed by its bad ar-
chitecture, and the want of ornaments ; the
walls are formed of pieces of timber, erected at two feet diftance, which fupport the
roof, and between thefe timbers the fpace
is filled up with a kind of lime-flate.
The church has no fteeple, its roof is flat,
and above this roof a bell is fixed in the
open air.   Moft of the country around this
bay belongs to the Prieft, who lets it to
the farmers.

The inhabitants chiefly live by agri-
culture, and the profits arifing from their
commerce in tar, which they extract from
the red pine, by making an incifion into
the tree in the fpring of the year, when the
fap is rifing, and before the tree has ftopped
running, it will produce feveral gallons of
turpentine, which they eafily manufacture
into tar.

It

It may be conjectured, that the country fituated upon the bay of this river being low, it was originally part of the bottom of the river, and was formed either by the decreafe of water, or increafe of earth, carried from the brooks, or thrown on it by ftorms, as a great part of the plants that grow here are marine. But in order fully to inform myfelf whether it was really as I apprehended, I enquired of feveral of the inhabitants, if ever they had found any fhells in digging, who anfwered, that they had never met with any thing but different kinds of earth and fand.

There is one thing very remarkable, of which we had a proof: the wind is generally different in the bay to what it is in the river, for upon failing into the bay we had as favourable a wind as could blow, but in the moment of entrance, it was directly the reverfe, which is thus acounted for : the bay being furrounded on all fides,

except

except one, with high mountains, and covered with tall woods, when the wind comes from the river, it ftrikes againft fome of thefe mountains, where it is repelled, and confequently takes an oppofite direction.

The people who inhabit this bay, as likewife thofe fettled lower down the river, feem very poor; they have the neceffaries of life in abundance, but debar themfelves of the comforts that fhould arife from them, living chiefly upon bread and milk, and carrying their other provifions, fuch as butter, cheefe, flefh, poultry, eggs, &c. to market, where having difpofed of them, they purchafe cloaths, brandy, and dreffes for the women. Yet notwithftanding their *pauvre* manner of living, they are always chearful and in high fpirits.

Our object on going on fhore was not fo much to gratify our curiofity, as to procure

procure fome vegetables; and as the Captain of the fhip could not fpeak a word of French, as indifferent a Frenchman as you know me to be, I was obliged to be the interpreter on this occafion. I however made the inhabitants underftand me very well, till I afked for fome potatoes, by the ufual fchool term of *pommes de terre*, and by which I underftand they are called in France; yet, notwithftanding the Canadians are allowed to fpeak as pure French as at Paris, I could not make them comprehend what it was I wanted, the man continually faying, *Monfieur, je fuis bien faché de ne pouvoir comprendre ce que vous fouhaitez*; at the fame time expreffing great uneafinefs, as I repeatedly affured him, *que j'etois bien fur qu'il en avoit*, which feemed to vex him ftill more. However, in walking over his plantation, I happened to fee a parcel in the corner of a fhed; pointing to them I faid, *Voila ce que je demande*, upon which, with great

great joy in his countenance, he exclaimed, *Oh! Monſieur, ce ſont des putat, putat*; adding, with great heartineſs, *Qu'il etoit bien aiſe d'etre en etat de me ſatisfaire.* Upon my telling him, in England we called them *pommes de terre*, he added, with a remark which I ſhould not have expected, *Que ce nom leur convenoit mieux que tout autre.* As I paid him very liberally for the vegetables we had of him, he ſaid, with great expreſſion of gratitude, *Ah! Monſieur, je me ſouviendrai toujours de vos bontés et des pommes de terre.*

Canada, from the fertility of its ſoil, and the ſalubrity of its climate, you would naturally imagine, contributed greatly to its own proſperity; but theſe, as in moſt other ſituations, are counterbalanced by its diſadvantages. Canada has only one river for its exports and imports, and even this is ſo blocked up with ice, as not to be navigable

gable during fix months, while heavy fogs
render the navigation flow and difficult
the remainder of the year. And although
the produce of Canada is fuperior to that
of the other provinces, ftill the latter, not
having fimilar impediments to encounter,
will always have a decided advantage over
this, in the convenience of almoft uninter-
rupted navigation.

The farm houfes are moftly built of
timber, confifting of three or four rooms,
and in one they have an iron ftove, which
is rendered fo hot, as to communicate fufficient warmth to the reft. The roofs
are covered with boards, and the crevices
and chinks of the timbers are filled with
clay, and their out buildings are thatched
with ftraw.

Below the bay of Gafpey there is an
ifland, called *Ifle Percée*; on your approach
to it, it has the appearance of the frag-
ment

ment of an old wall, being a steep rock of
about thirty fathoms in length, ten in
heighth, and four in breadth, which the
pilot told us was reported formerly to have
joined *Mont Joli*, which stands opposite to
it upon the Continent. This rock has in
the center of it an opening, in the form of
an arch (through which a small schooner
might pass in full sail); from which circumstance, you will easily imagine, it derives its name of *Isle Percée*.

The last object that attracts your attention before you enter the harbour of Quebec, is the isle of Orleans, a most beautiful large island, situated in the middle of
the river St. Laurence. It is seven leagues
and a half long, and two broad, in the
widest part, very high, with shores extremely steep and woody, though in some
places there is a gradual descent to the
river, and where that is the case, it is entirely free from woods, and upon these
                                                    spots

ſpots there are farm houſes cloſe to the ſhore.

The iſle itſelf is well cultivated, and the eye is continually amuſed with large ſtone houſes, corn fields, meadows, paſtures and woods, with the addition of ſeveral good ſtone churches, ſome of which ſtand ſo cloſe to the river, and it being Sunday when we paſſed the iſland, that we heard them at maſs.

The river St. Laurence, till you come to this iſland, is moſtly four or five leagues in breadth, but after you paſs it, ſuddenly narrows, ſo as to be no more than a mile broad at Quebec, and from which circumſtance this city derives its name, from the Indian word Quebeio, or Quebec, which ſignifies a ſtrait or narrowing.

Shortly after we had paſſed this iſland, and turned Point Levy; we entered the harbour,

harbour, which has the appearance of a large bay, for Point Levy ftretches itfelf out towards the Ifle of Orleans, fo as to hide the fouth channel; and that ifland projects fo as to conceal the north.

On entrance, you are ftruck with the grandeur and confufion and variety of objects that prefent themfelves: fronting is the city; on the right is the beautiful fall of Montmorency, and a view up the river St. Charles; on the left there is an extenfive view up the river St. Laurence, and over the falls of Montmorency; a delightful profpect of feveral leagues round the country, interfperfed with the villages of Beauport, Charlebourg, &c. a particular account of which I fhall give you in my next.

I am, yours, &c.

LET-

LETTER VI.

Quebec, October 27th, 1776.

MY DEAR FRIEND,

IN my defcription of this province, you muft not expect a tirefome detail of diftances, or a romantic defcription of the country, but a few general obferva-tions, as I fhall pafs through the different parts of it, which are deferving notice.

This city, the capital of Canada, from the fingularity of its fituation, boafts of having that which no other city in the known world poffeffes, a frefh water har-bour, an hundred and twenty leagues from

VOL. I. E the

the fea, capable of containing an hundred
fhips of the line; it is built in the form of
an amphitheatre, on the declivity of a pe-
ninfula, formed by the rivers St. Laurence
and St. Charles, and commands a profpect
over extenfive fields, which appears rich,
lively and beautiful.

This city fuffered fo much during the
long fiege, laft winter, that it will by no
means anfwer the beautiful defcription
given by that elegant writer Mrs. Brookes,
in her Emily Montague, for many houfes
were deftroyed for fuel, others to prevent
harbouring the enemy, and fhot and fhells
continually defacing and burning the reft,
you muft eafily imagine, greatly contribute
to deftroy all ideas of regularity.

The city is divided into two towns, diftinguifhed by the *upper* and the *lower*,
which, during the fiege, were feparated by a
                                        ftrong

ftrong ftockade, which proved extremely fortunate for us, as the enemy got into the lower town, but not being able to keep poffeffion, they fet it on fire, and nearly deftroyed the whole of it.

There are two communications from the lower to the upper town, the one for carriages, by a ferpentine road up a very fteep afcent, and the other for foot paffengers, up a flight of fteps cut out of the rock.

The carriage road to the upper town, as well as the ftreets in general, are almoft impaffable for either man or beaft, never having been paved fince the fiege, when the pavement was entirely torn up, that the fhells might bury themfelves in the ground before they burft, whereby they were rendered lefs dangerous.

The diftreffes of the inhabitants in a befieged town, at all times are very great;

E 2   but

but here they were rendered particularly fo, from the extreme feverity of the weather, being deprived of fuel, and compelled to refide in their cellars, as the only place that could afford them the leaft fhelter.

The Governor's houfe ftands upon an high eminence, and being bomb-proof, the family thought themfelves in perfect fecurity: from its elevation too, it was imagined to be out of the reach of cannon fhot. One evening, however, they were rather unpleafantly convinced of their error, by a fhot paffing through an adjoining room to that in which they were playing at cards; this threw them into no little confufion, and obliged them to retire to that part of the houfe in which the other inhabitants were compelled to refide.

You may remember, fome months before my departure from England, that Mr.

Mr. W---, who is a *bon vivant*, jocularly remarked, if he were confined to any single room, it fhould be the cellar; he was then at the Governor's, enjoying his favourite wifh, happy as good company and good wine could make him, the found of every cannon being the fignal for a bumper.

A Major who was here during the fiege, expreffed his aftonifhment to me that the place held out fo long, having an amazing feverity of weather, and numberlefs other difficulties to encounter; and that its fafety was entirely owing to the great exertions of General Carleton, who continually encouraged the inhabitants to action, for they chiefly compofed the ftrength of the garrifon.

The fuburb of *St. Fauxbourg* is entirely deftroyed, but that, as well as the lower town, is now rebuilding, and when compleated, muft add greatly to the beauty of.

E 3   the

the city. There are feveral quays, and a convenient place for heaving down fhips to be repaired, called *Cul de Sac*, where the King's fhips lay up during the winter, to preferve them from danger upon the freezing and breaking up of the ice, which is more hazardous than you can imagine; for unlefs the fhips are got into this *Cul de Sac* in proper time, they are very much damaged, and fometimes totally loft, by the amazing iflands of ice that float down the river.

This city is at prefent badly accommo- dated as to taverns, there being but one in the upper, and another in the lower town, both of them in the worft ftate imaginable; for although they provide good dinners, the reft of the accommodations are fuch as would difgrace the meaneft public-houfe in London. No attendance whatever from fervants; no feperate apartments, and fifteen or twenty people are obliged to fleep sleep in one room, about a yard apart from each other; usually deprived of natural rest in such vile dormitories, one scarcely feels refreshed the whole day, and let me assure you, since I have been here, I have not enjoyed a good night's repose, from the sonorous music I am surrounded with, arising from that natural and almost universal wind instrument, the nose. The owners of these taverns imagine, if they give good dinners and good wine, they perform wonders. This, however, may be said in their favour, as to accommodation, that this city has been for many months past in a very deranged state, owing to the late siege.

The Canadians of the higher class are very polite and attentive to strangers; a few days since, I was invited to dine with one of the principal merchants, *chez Monsieur Roberdeau*; the dinner was entirely after the French fashion, and displayed

polite Canadians

with

with much taſte, but ſuch was the per-
verſeneſs of my Engliſh ſtomach, that it
could not reliſh one of their made diſhes;
and although I endeavoured to eat, out of
compliment, the maſter of the houſe perceived I did not do it with any guſto; he
then ſaid, *Ah! Monſieur, vous ne faites que
d'arriver dans ce pays; quand vous aurez été
avec nous un certain tems, vous aimerez beaucoup notre cuiſine. Je ſuis bien faché que dans
ce moment il ne ſe trouve rien a votre gout,
mais quand vous me ferez l'honneur de venir
une autrefois chez moi, j'aurai ſoin d'avoir du
ROAST BEEF et du PLUMB PUDDING que les
Anglois aiment tant.* When the deſert came,
whichwas before the cloth was removed, I
made amends for my not being able to eat
at dinner, which the maſter of the houſe
obſerving, ſaid, *Ah! Monſieur, ce n'eſt pas
que vous ne vous ſouciez pas des viandes, mais
c'eſt que vous etes un peu comme les enfans,
vous aimez les friandiſes;* when, fearful leſt
I ſhould be diſpleaſed at his raillery, with
a polite

a politenefs truly French, he filled his glafs, and added, *Allons; Monſieur, verſez et vive le Roi d'Angleterre.*

Fearful of lofing the opportunity that now prefents itſelf of conveying this to England, I have but juſt time fubfcribe myſelf,

Yours, &c.

LET-

LETTER   VII,

Quebec, October 30th, 1776.

MY DEAR FRIEND,

THE hafty conclufion I was obliged to put to my laft, having prevented me from entering fo fully into the defcription of this city as I had intended, I now tranf-mit to you fome further particulars rela-tive to its fiege, and the religion of its in-habitants.

The caufeway by which General Mont-gomery made his attack, is not more than twenty-four feet wide; on one fide is a lofty perpendicular rock, and on the other a fteep precipice, without any fence, down

to

to the river; this caufeway was defended by two ftrong barriers, and were I induced to give an opinion, nothing but a defperate effort could juftify the attack.   The event fatally proved it; for upon the advance of the enemy, the firft barrier was abandoned, which, after they had broke down, flufhed with fuccefs, and the hopes of eafily gaining the upper town, they rufhed on (with an intrepidity that might expect every thing from their valor) to the fecond barrier, where two pieces of cannon were concealed, and upon their approach were immediately fired, when great numbers of them were killed and wounded, and in their retreat many fell down the precipice; this defeat greatly contributed to put an end to the fiege, the termination of which, had nearly been fruftrated, by the eager impetuofity of the failors, who were pofted with thofe guns, as they could fcarcely be reftrained from firing them when the enemy attacked the

firft

firft barrier, which, if they had done, the flaughter would not have been fo great, nor the enemy perhaps have loft their brave Commander. But by the threats of the officers upon duty at that poft, the guns were not fired till the enemy were within a few yards of them; and as they advanced abreaft, as many as the caufeway would admit of, you may eafily conceive what havoc there muft have been amongft them.

In this daring enterprize fell a man, who lived long enough to eftablifh a reputation, *Nec poterit ferrum, nec edax abolere vetuftas, quod nec Jovis ira nec ignis,* as no doubt it will be handed down by the Americans to the lateft ages. He died too foon for the fupport of that unnatural faction, to which, from miftaken principles, he was deeply attached; and being a man worthy of fome notice, you fhall know the little hiftory I have been able to collect of him.

In

In the laſt war he was an officer in our
ſervice, and diſtinguiſhed himſelf in ſeveral
inſtances. At the peace he came over to
this country, and married an American
lady, where by his conduct and agreeable
manners, he was reſpected as much as if
he had been a native; and being, from his
marriage and long reſidence in the country,
conſidered as a man fit to be truſted with a
command, he was appointed Brigadier General by the Congreſs; this commiſſion he
wiſhed to decline, feeling a compunction,
as a native of Great Britain, and once in
the King's ſervice, to bear arms againſt
his Sovereign. His wavering inclination
was unfortunately ſubdued, by the over-
perſuaſion of a fond wife, whom he loved
moſt affectionately, and the importunate
ſolicitation of his relations and friends.
When he had taken a decided part, his
conduct fully correſponded with the high
opinion that had been formed of his abilities and fidelity. No one who lived ſo
ſhort

fhort a time in their employ, could render
them more important fervices, or do their
caufe more honor.

When he had been induced to facrifice
the happinefs he enjoyed in private life,
and enter into the fervice of the Congrefs,
he was then abfolved from all views ad-
verfe to their party (of which he had been
fufpected) and confidered as a man who
took a part in the caufe from confcience
and principle. In this light he was viewed
while living, and fpoken of when dead. He
had the fingular felicity of being equally
efteemed by the friends and foes of the
party he efpoufed; the latter acknowledged his worth, though they reprobated the
caufe in which he fell. To the praife of
General Carleton, his remains were, by
the General's order, interred with all military honors.

An

Very fhortly after this repulfe, an
American foldier, in attempting to ftep
out of his *batteaux*, at Wolfe's Cove, fell
into the water, and catching hold of a
flake of ice that was floating down the
river, he got upon it, and was carried
down the ftream.   As he paffed Quebec
clofe to the fhore, he was feen by a centinel, who obferving a man in diftrefs,
called out for help, when numbers flew to
his affiftance, and found him motionlefs;
by the help of fpirituous liquors, with
fome difficulty they brought him to life for
a moment, and juft recovering fpeech
enough to tell them, that the city would
not long be in our poffeffion, he inftantly
expired.

A mile from the city is a Convent, that
was once poffeffed of a beautiful garden,
but this, as well as their chapel, with the
images and other ornaments of their religion, are greatly injured.   The enemy,
after

after taking poffeffion of the Convent, converted it into an hofpital, and com- pelled the nuns to attend upon their fick and wounded; and what was ftill more perfecuting to their religion than to their wifhes, feveral of the nuns, after they had abandoned it, proved capable of in fome meafure making up for the ravages of war, by producing what may in future become the ftrength and fupport of their country.

There are feveral churches in each town, but thofe in the upper are the moft mag- nificent, and have fuftained the leaft da- mage. The largeft of thefe churches, and what may be termed the cathedral, has nothing worthy of notice, except a hand- fome fteeple; it is entirely roofed with flate, and is the only building I obferved that has this advantage, they being all covered with fhingles. It is much orna- mented in the infide; the gallery is bold, light,

light, and well wrought, furrounded with an iron balluftrade, painted and gilt, of curious workmanfhip; one thing, however, appears very fingular, that the pulpit is likewife gilt, and feems to have had more labor beftowed *upon*, than it is ever likely to have *within* it; there are three altars handfomely defigned, and fome good pictures; it is without any dome or cupola, having only a flat ceiling, very curioufly ornamented; it is not as in moft Cathedrals, paved with ftone, but floored with planks, which makes this church the more fupportable in winter; in others you are generally ftarved to death with cold. After the Romifh fervice is over, on a Sunday, the Governor, with the officers and foldiers of the garrifon, and the Proteftant inhabitants of the city, refort thither to their worfhip. This little circumftance I mention to you, as the paffing of the Quebec bill made fuch a noife in England; clearly to fhew there is no animosity among the inhabitants, on the score of religion. Where the Canadians, who constitute the principal part of the inhabitants of this province, did not interfere with our religion, I cannot but think it was a very necessary and politic step in Government to tolerate theirs; as at the time the bill passed, it was judged proper to make this sacrifice to them, in order to gain their affections, which seemed to be wavering, whether they should not join the other provinces in rebellion against England.

For my own part, I am led to imagine, from the conversation I have had with several of the principal inhabitants, they never were in the least apprehensive of their religion being suppressed, but that idea was instilled into their minds by some party at home, who, I am sorry to observe, are more dangerous than any enemy we can possibly have abroad.

With

With all the advantages of the laws of our conftitution, the toleration of their religion, and the bleffings of liberty, the Canadians are by no means well affected to the Englifh Government, but have a ftrong propenfity to be under the protection of the French; and, I am confident, would affift the Americans, had we not fuch a powerful force in this province.

believe that Canadians would have helped the Americans

The garrifon of this city, and a few inhabitants at Montreal, are ftaunch to the interefts of Government; for their fidelity and courage have been proved; upon the commencement of the fiege, the General ordered every one out of the city, that he could entertain the leaft fufpicion of, none of whom have fince made their appearance.

The army is now returning from the Lakes, and at prefent the garrifon confifts of Colonel Maclean's regiment, and the

recruits

recruits lately arrived from England; the 34th regiment is daily expected, as the army is getting into winter quarters. General Carleton and General Burgoyne are both here, the latter of whom fails for England in a few days.

My friend Captain W---n, who is embarking for that country where my fondeſt wiſhes are placed, will deliver you this: he has juſt called upon me for my letters. I muſt therefore conclude. You ſhall hear from me by the lateſt ſhip that ſails.

Yours, &c.

LET-

L E T T E R   VIII.

Quebec, Nov. 4th, 1776,

MY DEAR FRIEND,

VISITING two or three of the villages round this city, has enabled
me to give you some little defcription of
the country and its inhabitants.

About Charlebourg and Beauport it is
rather *champaign,* but becomes more woody
towards Lorette.   The farm houfes interfperfed about the country are very numerous, and being generally whitened on
the outfide, form a neat and picturefque
appearance : their houfes moftly confift of
one floor, very few having a ftory to them,
which gives rife to the idea, that the Ca-

F 3   nadians

nadians will *tell* a ſtory well, though they never *make* one.

You would be pleaſed to find them extremely neat in their houſes, very attentive to their cattle, and careful of the ſtock on their farms. They are at preſent employed in cutting and getting in wood for the winter, for themſelves and the market, for though it is ſo early, there has been a ſevere fall of ſnow ; wood-cutting continues all this month, and in December, when the winter is ſet in, it is carried into the city upon ſleighs over the ſnow, being a much eaſier conveyance than with carts, as the roads are ſo intolerably bad.

The Canadians in general are a ſwarthy people, and low in ſtature ; their dreſs conſiſts of a kind of jacket, and when the weather is cold, a blanket coat, which they faſten round them with a worſted ſaſh. They moſtly wear a woollen cap, but

but in the cold weather a fur one, and have amazing long queues, of which they are exceedingly proud. They are feldom or ever found without a pipe in their mouths, a habit which they acquire in their very infancy. I was much furprized upon going into one of their houfes, in which there was a large family, moftly boys, to find, that from the youngeft up to the father, they all fmoaked; nay, one of three years old had a pipe in his mouth. Their ufual mode of living being chiefly milk and vegetables, which, joined to the number of the faft days impofed on them by their religion, renders them a very meagre and flender people.

The women are extremely lively, good-natured and obliging, and very neat in their perfons, but have not the leaft pretenfion to beauty. The men are far from agreeable, for fince they have enjoyed the bleffings of an Englifh Government, they

F 4   are

are become infolent and overbearing, eafily
offended, and when they fancy themfelves
fo, their cry is, *Je vais le dire au General
Carleton*; and the General is of that good-
natured, affable difpofition, that he always
liftens to their complaints, and is continually plagued and tormented with fome
of the moft trivial nature, by thefe troublefome and tenacious people, for they conceive their Governor is bound to hear
them, efpecially their *Seigneurs*, or Lords
of the village; it is a title you have not
among you, but I affure you thofe who
poffefs it here, fancy themfelves of no little
importance, and affume more confequence
than the firft peer in England.

These *Seigneurs* are defcendants of thofe
officers and gentlemen who firft fettled, and
had grants in this province, when Canada
was only a vaft foreft; who, not being proper perfons to cultivate it themfelves, nor
poffeffed of a fufficient fund to pay labour-
ers,

ers, let out the grounds at a very flender quit rent; fo that with the fines, which were here very fmall, and what is called the *Droit du Moulin, & Metairie*, a lord-fhip, which confifts of two leagues in front, and an unlimited depth, can yield them no great revenue; and there are many planters on their manors, who by their induftry have become wealthier than the owner himfelf; notwithftanding which they ftand in great awe of thefe *Seigneurs*, as they are defcended from an-tient nobility in France, the forefathers of whom were permitted by Louis XIV. to exercife commerce as well by fea as land, without queftion, interruption, or dero-gating from their quality and rights; and to you, who fo well know the French, I need not fay in what manner any one de-fcended from nobility conduɛts himfelf, and the *hauteur* he treats every one with.

About

About three leagues from this city is a
nation of Indians, who live at a ſmall village called Indian Lorette : they are quite
civilized, have a church, go regularly
to maſs, and are extremely ingenious in
making bead ornaments.

Theſe Indians, who are really Chriſtians,
of the Romiſh perſuaſion, have a chapel
built nearly on the model, and of the ſame
dimenſions as that I have heard you relate
you met with in Italy, of *Santa Caſa*, and,
as in that, have an image of the Virgin,
which, upon enquiry, appears to be a copy
of that very ſtatue. Whether it was the
effect of imagination, devotion, or of any
other cauſe, I cannot ſay, but upon attending the chapel, I was ſeized with an
inward and ſacred terror, of which I can
give no account. The ſolid piety of
the Indians, (whom we are taught to believe ſo naturally ferocious, as no edifi-
cation, religious or moral, can overcome)
added,

added to the gloomy horror of the fituation, made a violent impreffion upon me,
which became the more ftrong, upon obferving the fervor and modefty which they
difplayed in their devotions.

Thefe Indians had a great number
of dogs with them, which feems to be
the only domeftic animal they breed;
they are trained up for hunting, and
are equal to any hounds; appearing
to be all of one fpecies, having upright
ears, of dark brindled color, with a long
fnout, like that of a wolf. None of our
Englifh dogs are more remarkable for their
fidelity, which is rather to be wondered at,
being but very ill fed, and never careffed
by them.

As hereafter, and no doubt before my
return to England, I fhall meet with many
Indians of different nations, cuftoms and
manners,

manners, give me leave to make a few reflections upon thefe favages, as they are
called, and civilized man.

In regard to the former, their origin
and antiquity is quite uncertain; the only
matter, therefore, to be confidered is, whether thefe untutored nations are more or
lefs happy than us? Whether they, who
are in the condition of man left to mere
animal inftinct, paffing their lives in hunting, feeding, producing their fpecies, and
repofing themfelves, do not pafs a life of
more felicity than ours, who can enjoy
every luxury of life, and vary our indulg-
ences and wants in a thoufand ways?

It is in our nature and difpofitions, that
we muft look for the means of happinefs.
Wherein then does it confift? Prefent fubfiftence, and (which I think there can be
none fo hardened as not to have) a thought
of futurity, and the hopes of enjoying
every

bleffing that is attendant on it. The favage never is in want; he lays in no ftores,
becaufe the earth and waters are refervoirs
to fupply them. Fifh and game are to be
had all the year. The favage has no houfe
to fecure him from the inclemency of the
external air, or commodious fire places, his
furs anfwering all thefe purpofes. His
labor is but for his own benefit; he fleeps
when he is weary, and is a ftranger to reftlefs nights. Little does he experience
wearinefs that arifes from unfatisfied de-
fires, or that uneafinefs of mind which
fprings from prejudice or vanity. As far as
I can perceive, the Indian is fubject to no
evils but thofe inflicted by nature.

In what manner then do we enjoy a
greater happinefs? Our food may be more
wholefome and delicate, our cloaths may
be fofter, and our habitations fecure us
better againft the weather; but then obferve the common people, who are the fup-

port of civil society; the number of men
who in all states bear the burthen of labor;
can they be said to be happy, who, by the
luxury and police of their governments,
are reduced to a state of servitude? And
to what outrages are those in a higher
sphere exposed to? If you are possessed of
any property, you know not how far it
may be called your own, but must, in all
probability, divide the produce between the
lawyer, in teaching you how to preserve it,
and the collector, who comes to levy unlimited taxes. If you have no property,
how can you be assured of a permanent
subsistence? What industry or invention
is secure against the vicissitudes of fortune,
or the encroachment of others.

In the forests of America, if there is any
scarcity in the north, the savages bend their
course to the south; but in our civilized
states, we are confined within certain limits, where if famine, or war, or pestilence,
with

a philosophe

with all their concomitant horrors, fhould befal us, all muft participate.

It certainly is apparent to every one, that injuftice prevails in the partial diftribution of fortunes and ftations, which muft be the effect and the caufe of oppreffion. In vain does cuftom, prejudice, ignorance, or hard labor, ftupify thofe of the lower clafs, fo as to render them infenfible of their degradation ; it is not in the power of religion or morality to hinder them from feeing and feeling the arrangements of policy, in the diftribution of what we call good and evil ; and, no doubt, you muft have often heard a poor man expoftulating with heaven, " What have I done, that I fhould deferve to be born in fuch an indigent and dependent fituation ?"

The reafon we prefer our condition to that of the favages is, becaufe civilization

has

has rendered us incapable of bearing fome
natural hardfhips, which they can endure;
and fimply that we are attached to fome
indulgence cuftom has made neceffary to
us. As a proof of this affertion, and how a
civilized man may habituate himfelf to the
fociety of favages, and return to this ftate
of nature, let me relate the fituation of a
Scotchman, who was caft away upon the
Ifland of *Fernandez*, where he lived alone;
his only enjoyments confifted in fupplying
his wants, and to fuch a pitch had his ideas
of happinefs raifed themfelves, that he forgot his country, his language, his name,
and even the articulation of words.   And
after a banifhment of four years, from the
burthens of focial life, he had loft all
thought of the paft, or anxiety for the
future.

One of the firft principles we imbibe,
one of the firft inftincts of man, is a
confcioufnefs of independence; and no
doubt

doubt but you muſt have obſerved, that the man who poſſeſſes a competent ſubſiſtence is incomparably happier than the rich man, who is reſtrained by prejudices and faſhions, which inceſſantly are reminding him of the loſs of his liberty, and which too frequently are the occaſion of the raſh and fatal act of ſuicide.

In comparing the ſtate of the ſavages to that of children, the queſtion may eaſily be decided, which has been ſo warmly in debate among the moſt learned men, "whether the ſtate of nature has the advantage over that of ſocial life?" And you, no doubt, will readily allow, that your ſtate of childhood, notwithſtanding the reſtraint of education, was the happieſt period of your life. Nothing ſurely can more clearly indicate the happineſs that children feel, than that habitual chearfulneſs they demonſtrate, when not under the ſchoolmaſter's rod.

VOL. I. G After

After all, a fingle word may determine this great queftion. Let us afk the civilized man if he is happy; and the favage whether he is unhappy? If they both anfwer in the negative, there is an end of the difpute.

How mortifying muft this parallel be to civilized nations? And the more painful the reflection, as it awakens the feelings to the caufe of their fufferings; no doubt but they will one time or other be convinced from whence it arifes---from the confufion of their opinions, from the defects of their political conftitutions, and from the capricioufnefs of their laws, which ever are in continual oppofition to the laws of nature. But for fear you think I am growing too fententious, I fhall return to my defcription of this province.

The

The woods of Canada abound with a large kind of rabbits, which are of a brown color in the fummer, and turn white in the winter, one of the effects of the extreme cold or fnow that prevails in this climate ; we found likewife vaft quantities of partridges, much larger than ours, which the Canadians call pheafants ; there are two forts of them, the fpruce and the pine : the meat of the former is very delicious, to thofe who are fond of the flavor of the fpruce. The market at this place is well fupplied with all kind of provifion, fifh and vegetables in abundance.

The place beft adapted to repay the labours of the hufbandman, are pointed out to him by the fpontaneous productions of nature; where the pine, the fir-tree, and the cedar grow folitarily, there he finds only watry and fandy grounds : but wherever the foil is covered with maple, oak, beech, yoke, elm, hickory, and fmall

　　　　　　　cherry-

cherry-trees, there he is certain to meet with a reward for his trouble of clearing away the woods, and may expect a great increase, without the difficulty of manuring.

Being informed that the pacquet fails this afternoon, and having several other letters to write, a further account of this province must be delayed till my next; and in hopes you will pardon my breaking off so abruptly, and leaving you in a state of suspence, I remain,

Yours, &c.

LET-

L E T T E R IX.

Quebec, November 5th, 1776.

MY DEAR FRIEND,

OBLIGED to conclude my laſt rather haſtily, I ſhall reſume my obſervations on this province, without any apology.

Moſt of the plantations in Canada are ſufficient to ſupply the wants of their reſpective owners, and there are few of them that do not yield rye, maize, barley, flax, hemp, tobacco, pulſe and pot-herbs, in great abundance, and thoſe of an excellent quality.

It

It is capable of furnifhing many articles for a trade with the Weſt Indies, which was wholly neglected, whilſt this province was under the French Government ; but ſince in our poſſeſſion, great quantities of flour, planks, and timber, proper for build-ing, have been exported to them : and as there is perhaps no country in the whole world which produces more ſorts of wood, or of a better quality, you may eaſily judge what immenſe riches may be drawn from thence, it conſiſting principally of woods.

I know not whether giving you an ac-count of the extenſive foreſts of Canada, will afford you any entertainment ; but when I inform you that they have the ap-pearance of being as ancient as the world itſelf, and were never planted by the hand of man, I think you will find ſome amuſe-ment in the deſcription of them.

On

On my firſt arrival in this country, I was ſtruck with the loftineſs of the pines, fir-trees, and cedars, which are of a ſize perfectly aſtoniſhing. There are two ſorts of pine, both of them yielding turpentine. The white pines produce, on their upper extremities a kind of muſhroom, which the Canadians adminiſter in caſes of the dyſentery. The red pines contain more turpentine, are heavier, and do not grow to ſuch a thickneſs; but where they flouriſh, the land is reckoned very good to raiſe corn.

There are ſeveral ſpecies of fir-trees, which riſe to a great height, are excellently calculated for maſts, as well as every ſort of carpenter's work.

There are two ſorts of cedars too, the white and red, the former of which grows the thickeſt, and the odour is in its leaves; whereas, in the latter, the odour is in the

wood,

wood, and far more agreeable. Of thefe
trees the Canadians make palings, but
moftly fhingles for covering their houfes,
from its extreme lightnefs.

*Cedars for
Shingles*

All over Canada are two forts of oak;
the white grows in low fwampy grounds,
the red in dry fandy lands.

There are three forts of walnuts; the
hard, the foft, and another with a thin bark.
The hard fort bear a fmall nut, very good
to eat, but apt to occafion coftivenefs, the
wood of which is only fit to burn. The
tender bears a large fruit, with a hard fhell,
the kernels of which are excellent: the
wood of this tree is fingularly curious,
being almoft incorruptible in water or in
the ground, and difficult to confume
in the fire: of this wood the Canadians
make their coffins. The third fort produces a nut which is exceedingly bitter,
but

but yields an excellent oil, ufed by the inhabitants for their lamps.

Beech and elm trees are in great abundance; and in the thickeft woods are found
vaft numbers of cherry and plumb-trees.

There are an infinite number of others,
but as I am no Botanift, you will pardon
my giving an account of what is here in
fuch variety, that perfons who have taken
the moft unremitting pains to difcover
them, have not been capable of defcribing
half their number, I fhall conclude this
heavy detail of trees, with that of the
maple, which boafts of many excellent
qualities.

The maple tree yields in great quantities
a liquor which is cool and refrefhing, with
an agreeable flavor. The Canadians make
a fugar of it, a very good pectoral,
and ufed for coughs. There are many
trees

trees that yield a liquor they can convert into fugar, but none in fuch abundance as the maple. You will no doubt be furprized to find, in Canada, what Virgil predicted of the Golden Age, *Et dura quercus fudabunt rofcida mella.*

The ftock of the farming part of the inhabitants in this province, confifts generally of about a fcore or two of fheep, ten or twelve cows, and five or fix oxen for the plough; the cattle are fmall but excellent, and the people, fince they have been under the Englifh Government, live in a degree of eafe and happinefs unknown to the country people in England, and are now improving their farms and enriching themfelves very faft. Before the commencement of the war, they ufed to export vaft quantities of wheat and all forts of grain, to the other provinces and the Weft India iflands; but when under the French Government, they were fo opprefled by their

Seigneurs,

Seigneurs, that they never raifed more grain than would ferve themfelves and the ftock on their farms; whenever they did, it was generally claimed by the *Seigneurs* for the ufe of Government. The Canadians were at that time a very indolent fet of people: now they reap the fweets of their induftry, and are quite the reverfe.

I went yefterday to view the Fall of Montmorency, which is really beautiful. The breadth of it is not above ten or twelve yards, and its perpendicular height one hundred and twenty feet; by the violent fall of fuch an immenfe body of water, there is always a thick fog of vapors, which occafions a continual rain, for fome diftance round the bottom. Anxious to examine it as minutely as poffible, I approached within twelve yards of the Fall, when a fudden guft of wind blew fuch a thick fog off the fpray, that in lefs than a minute I was as wet as if I had walked half

an

an hour in a heavy fhower, which, however, did not prevent my endeavouring to
fatisfy my curiofity, for I perfevered, in
hopes of accomplifhing my wifh, which,
like many of our ardent purfuits, did not
bring me that recompence I had flattered
myfelf it would; for having obtained the
purport of my intention, inftead of the
beautiful appearance I had pictured to my
imagination, to be difcerned between the
rock and the immenfe body of water that
was falling from fuch a prodigious height,
I found myfelf enveloped in a very thick
fog of fpray, fcarcely able to fee my hand
when extended, and where, in all probability, if I had continued five minutes, and
the wind changed, I was in danger of being
drowned. The noife occafioned by the fall
was fo great, that an officer who was with
me was obliged to fpeak as loud as he could,
to make me underftand any thing he faid.
It is fometimes heard at Quebec, which is
two leagues diftant to the fouthward, and
when

when that is the cafe, it is the fign of an
approaching ftrong north-eaft wind.

One thing remarkable is, that this plentiful fall of water, which never dries
up, one would imagine, muft proceed from
fome fine river : but it is quite the reverfe,
it being only a puny ftream, which in fome
places is fcarcely fufficient to cover the
ankle ; it flows, however, conftantly, and
derives its fource from a pleafant lake,
twelve leagues diftant from the falls.

I have vifited the plains of Abraham, to
fee the remains of the enemy's encampment, and could not help contrafting thofe
who had fo lately abandoned that place,
with the poffeffors of it when the brave
Wolfe fell! Nor was it poffible to fupprefs
a figh to the memory of that gallant officer,
who, at fo early a period in life, had acquired the efteem and admiration of all
mankind. While in the very arms of death,

he

added glory and conqueſt to the Britiſh empire.

Nor could I help lamenting, at the ſame time, the fate of an officer of conſiderable merit, though an enemy, the brave Montgomery, who commanded the troops that had ſo lately abandoned this encampment, and of whom I have already ſpoken: he poſſeſſed all the fire of military ardor, ruſhed with impatience in the front of every danger, and met his death, " e'en at the cannon's mouth," where he unfortunately fell a ſacrifice to miſtaken principles, unnatural rebellion, and the ambitious views of a few deſigning men.----His courage and death would have done honor to a better cauſe.

The people in this city are making preperations for the winter, and you would think it impoſſible they could conſume the amazing rafts of timber that are already floated

floated down the river; but I am informed they are a very inconfiderable part of
what are expected.---It is not in the leaft
furprizing they were obliged to pull down
houfes for fuel laft winter, during the
fiege.

Europeans muft form a terrible idea of
the intenfe cold of this country, from the
preparations the Canadians take to guard
againft it; for the inhabitants are pafting
paper round their windows, and every
crevice where they imagine the leaft cold
will penetrate.

Inftead of fire-places they make ufe of
iron ftoves, which muft be extremely un-
healthy; a few days fince I went into a
room when there was a fire in one of
them, and had not been there above five
minutes, when I was feized with a moft
intolerable head-ach, which I can only
attribute to the fulphureous air that pro-
ceeds

ceeds from thefe ftoves; and, for my own part, imagine they are the occafion of the Canadians having fuch fallow complexions; but cuftom, which in fome meafure over-comes all prejudices, will no doubt recon-cile me to them.

The fhips are all preparing to fail for England, left the river fhould freeze up.

I have been this afternoon upon the ramparts, to fee the Apollo frigate drop down, in which General Burgoyne fails for England; who, I am perfuaded, has the fincere and ardent wifhes of all ranks in the army, for his fafety and happy ar-rival. The General joins to the dignity of office, and ftrict attention to military difcipline, that confideration, humanity, and mildnefs of manners, which muft ever endear him to all who have the happinefs to be under his command; for my own part, I fhall pray with Shakefpear, " that

the

the winds of all the corners may kifs the fails, and make his veffel profperous."

I remained on the ramparts to take the laft look of the Apollo, who, with a fteady and favourable breeze, failed magnificently down the river, and was foon out of fight. You cannot guefs how it affected me; fhall I confefs that more than once I wifhed myfelf on board her: it was fuch a fight as muft awaken the mind to all its natural attachments. But that I may not think too much of country and friends, at this time, I fhall haftily conclude myfelf,

Yours, &c.

L E T T E R   X.

Montreal, November 16*th,* 1776.

MY DEAR FRIEND,

AFTER a tedious march of near three weeks, which for a young foldier is a pretty good initiation into the toils of his profeffion, I am fafe arrived at this place.

As we could not march many miles in a day, through the feverity of the weather, bad roads, and the fhortnefs of the days, I am enabled to give you fome little defcription of the country between this city and Quebec.

Both

Both fides of the river are very well fettled, which affords a pleafing profpect. The farms moftly lie clofe to the water-fide, and at fome diftance from each other, fo that each farmer has his poffeffions entirely diftinct from thofe of his neighbour's. But ·had an edict, which was paffed in the year 1745, when this province was under the French Government, been obferved, it would have been one continued ftreet from Quebec to this place, as it forbade the Canadians from extending their plantations more than an acre and a half in front, and thirty or forty acres in depth; by which means indolent heirs would not have waited for the inheritance of their fathers, as they would have been under the neceffity of forming new plantations, and fuch vaft fpaces of wood would no longer have. feparated them from each other.

H 2 But

But whether that indolence they then
poffeffed proceeded from nature, or the
rigor of their Government, they feem now
to have entirely loft it, and are become
more induftrious; as I perceived, in many
places, they were clearing away the woods
to form new plantations.

Moft of the farm houfes are built of
ftone, confifting of three or four rooms,
which are heated with a ftove, nearly
upon the fame conftruction as thofe I
defcribed to you. Some of them have
orchards annexed, though in general they
are without fuch an accommodation, but
all have exceeding good kitchen gar-
dens.

Every three leagues there is a church,
with a kind of little village, confifting of
the parfonage, the *auberge*, the fchool for
boys and girls, and a few houfes belonging to tradefmen, thofe but few indeed,
and

and fo thinly fcattered, that it fcarcely
gives you the idea of a village. .Trade is
confidered by any defcendant of the *nobl ſſe*
a difgrace, yet there are few inhabitants
but what claim fome affinity to one *Seig-*
neur or another, who, though they think
it no derogation to plough, fow, and reap
upon their plantations, deem it ignominious in the extreme, to be a mechanic
or tradefman.   Notwithftanding which, I
was much furprized to find, that the
principal inhabitant in each village, who
generally belongs to fome *nobleſſe*, was the
poft-mafter, and kept the only *Auberge* in
the place; nay, did not think his nobility
offended, with providing horfes and entertaining travellers, which I remember to
have heard you fay is the cafe in many
parts of Italy.

Between each church, or village, there
are feveral croſſes put up on the road-fide,
parallel to the fhores of the river, and

H 3   which

which are common throughout Canada.
They are made of wood, about fifteen
or twenty feet high, and proportionably
broad : In that fide towards the road is a
fquare hole, in which they place fome
wax images, either of our Saviour on the
crofs, or of the holy Virgin, with the
child in her arms, and before that, a piece
of glafs to prevent its being injured by
the weather.   Thefe croffes are ornamented with all the inftruments they think
the Jews employed in crucifying our
Saviour, fuch as the hammer, tongs, nails,
a flafk of vinegar, with many more things
than one would fuppofe were really made
ufe of, or even invented; and frequently
the figure of a cock is placed at the top,
which appeared to me rather fingular, as
it could have not the leaft affinity to the
crucifixion, and muft rather be fuppofed
an allufion to the cock's crowing when
St. Peter denied our Saviour.

Thefe

These crosses, however good the intention of erecting them may be, are continually the causes of great delays in travelling, which to persons not quite so superstitiously disposed as the Canadians, are exceedingly unpleasant in cold weather; for whenever the drivers of the calashes, which are open, and nearly similar to your one horse chaises, come to one of them, they alight, either from their horses or carriage, fall on their knees, and repeat a long prayer, let the weather be ever so severe.

The usual mode of travelling is in these calashes: in the front of those which travel post, a man sits to drive, and who, let your business be of ever so great importance, will alight at these crosses, and pay his accustomed homage.

One day, on our march, being sent forward to procure quarters, with our friend

H 4   Cap-

Captain Grattan, whofe pleafantry of manners you are well acquainted with ; for expedition we went in a poft-calafh. The
weather was fo exceffively fevere, that with
the affiftance of fur coverings, we could
fcarcely keep ourfelves warm. Not above
a mile had been beguiled, before we came
to one of thefe croffes, when the fellow
who drove us ftopped ; upon afking him
why he did fo, he replied, *Ce n'eft que pour
faire une petite prière* ; which *petite prière*
he was nearly five minutes in repeating,
when he mounted his feat. We complained
of being almoft perifhed with cold, when
he replied, *Allons, allons, je vais me depêcher*,
and after taking two or three whiffs of his
pipe, whipped up his horfes, and made
amends for his ftopping. We had not
gone a mile and a half further, before
another crofs made its unwelcome appearance : here he muft alight, and *faire une
autre petite prière*, which, upon our not
confenting to, he begged we would let him
juft

juft ftop, *le tems de faire un figne de croix,*
which he was not long about.   We then
jogged on again with great chearfulnefs, as
he drove pretty faft; foon after we perceived the village to which we were deftined
for quarters, when again he fuddenly ftopt,
and upon our faying there was no crofs
there, he immediately cried out, *Mais en*
voici une la, which, being at fome diftance
from the road, we had not obferved, requefting us to let him halt but a moment:
Il faut que je defcende ici; c'eft mon village;
we told him he fhould not, and that he
muft drive into the village as faft as he
could.   Upon this he growled inwardly,
and complained openly, till he came oppofite to it, where he ftopped again;
before he could defcend, our friend Grattan laid hold of his long queue, of which
I told you they are exceedingly proud, and
declared, if he did not immediately drive
on, he would inftantly cut it off.----
This being afferted with fome degree of
warmth,

warmth, he thought fit to facrifice his religion to his vanity, fo juft croffing himfelf,
muttered a fhort prayer, and drove us as faft
as he could to the end of our journey,
facrant contre the Englifh officers ; and I do
not doubt, if one could form any idea from
his countenance, but he fent us both into
purgatory with fuch curfes, that all the
maffes which could be offered would not be
able to releafe us from it, for having treated
his religion and his queue with fo little
ceremony.

Leaving you to make your own reflections on thefe Canadians and their religion,
I remain,

Yours, &c.

Canadian drove them to village - stops
three times to pray at a cross - last time
they requested he not stop - he condemned
them to purgatory

LET-

LETTER XI.

Montreal, Nov. 20th, 1776.

MY DEAR FRIEND,

I SHALL now proceed with my obfervations, and the remainder of the occurrences which happened in our march from Quebec to this place.

About half way between Quebec and Montreal, is a town called *Trois Rivieres* ; it takes its name from three rivers, whofe currents join here, and fall into the river St. Laurence. Previous to my giving you any defcription of this place, permit me to relate a trifling circumftance that occurred,

juft

just as we entered the town. About half a mile before we came to it, so sudden and naufeous a scent affailed our olfactory nerves, as nearly to suffocate us, which lasted till we arrived at the outskirts.--- Upon enquiry, we found it arose from an animal, which the Canadians call the *Enfant du Diable*, or *bête puante*; a title which it derives from its ill scent, occafioned by difcharging his urine whenever he is attacked, and which infects the air for a great diftance. Laying afide this quality, it is in other refpects a beautiful creature, being about the fize of a cat, with a fine fhining fur, of a dark grey color, ftreaks of white gliftening from the head to the tail, which is bufhy, like that of a fox, and turned up as a fquirrel's: this had been purfued by fome dogs which the foldiers had with them, acrofs the road, but when it came near us, its ftench was almoft infupportable.

Thefe

These *Enfant du Diable* differ from your *Enfant du Diable*, the London beaux, who have all their prettyisms perhaps, but are *eternally* exhaling their peftiferous odours, fearful, if they referved them till *purfued*, they would have no opportunity to

" Taint the flying air, and ftink in ftate."

The country is pleafant, and there are feveral good houfes about the town, but they were greatly damaged by the Americans, upon abandoning it, after their defeat this fummer, when their army was routed, and feveral of their Generals, with great numbers of their men, taken prifoners. This place is the winter cantonments of the German troops, who are commanded by General Reidefel; he commands likewife the diftrict between Quebec and Montreal.

This town, by reafon of the three rivers, ufed to be much frequented by the feveral nations

nations of Indians, and was built with a view of encouraging trade with the northern ones in particular. It had every profpect of being the fecond city in the province, but the fur trade was foon diverted from this market, and carried entirely to Montreal, it being fome leagues nearer to the Indians; and though we have feveral trading places with them upon the lakes Ontario and Superior, Montreal will always fupport its confequence, as being the neareft and moft convenient place for fhipping the furs to England. *Trois Rivieres* has now loft all its traffic and is fupported chiefly by the travellers paffing between the two cities.

There are feveral churches, and two convents, the nuns of which are reckoned the moft ingenious of any in Canada, in all kinds of fancy ornaments, needle work, and curious toys.

During

During my ftay at *Trois Rivieres*, there came down from the *Illinois*, feveral Indians of that nation, with an interpreter, to acquaint us, that they would be down in the fpring, and would take up the hatchet in favor of "*their good Brother who refided beyond the great waters*." Among the groupe I obferved one, who had hanging round his neck the image of the holy Virgin, with our Saviour in her arms, which I thought very fingular, as he was of a nation efteemed extremely ferocious in their manner, and whom the French Miffionaries could not convert; but upon my enquiring of the interpreter if he knew the reafon, he gave me the following account:

In fome fkimirfh, when the *Illinois* were at war with the Canadians, this image had fallen into their hands, amongft other plunder.   Sometime afterwards as a Miffionary, of which the French had great
numbers

numbers travelling through the interior parts of Canada, to cultivate friendfhip, and eftablifh their religion among the Indians; by chance he met this perfon, and obferving the image, was very much aftonifhed; the manner in which he took notice of it, excited the curiofity of the poor favage, to know what it reprefented, when the Miffionary, who no doubt was pleafed to have fuch an opportunity of difplaying his religion, told him, that it reprefented the mother of his God, and that the child fhe held in her arms reprefented God himfelf, who had made himfelf man for the falvation of the human fpecies, and explaining to him the myftery of our incarnation, affuring him, that in all dangers the Chriftians addreffed themfelves to this holy mother, who feldom failed to extricate them. The Indian liftened with the utmoft attention to this difcourfe, and went away.

Some-

Being out a hunting, foon after this, juft as he had difcharged his piece at a deer, one of the *Outagami* Indians, whofe nation was at variance with the *Illinois*, and who was lying in ambufh, prefented his piece at his head. In this fituation he recollected what had been told him about the mother of God, and invoked her protection. The *Outagami* endeavoured to difcharge his piece, but miffed; he cocked a fecond time, and the fame thing happened five times fucceffively. In the interim the *Illinois* had loaded his piece, and prefented it to the *Outagami*, who chofe rather to furrender than be fhot. From that time the *Illinois* would never ftir from his village without his fafeguard, which he imagines renders him invulnerable. There can remain little doubt but this circumftance was the means of his converfion to Chriftianity, and the Romifh religion: for he has certainly embraced that perfuafion, as I followed him to the

VOL. I.   I   great

great church, where, upon his entrance, after croſſing himſelf with the holy water, he fell upon his knees, and ſeemed to wor-ſhip with as much devotion as the moſt devout of the Canadians. But to return to my deſcription of this place.

The road from Quebec hither is the whole way within ſight of the river, being moſtly upon its banks, which renders it extremely pleaſant to travellers, eſpecially in the ſummer, as there is a conſtant breeze.

The river from Quebec to *Trois Rivieres* is very wide, and at that place it forms a very large lake, called *St. Pierre*, where the eye cannot reach acroſs ; you can only diſcern a large body of water, with ſeveral iſlands, which, with the ſmall veſſels ſail-ing between them, form a very romantic proſpect. The tide comes no farther than this lake; terminating a few leagues

beyond

beyond *Trois Rivieres*, when you meet with the river again, where it runs extremely rapid, at the rate of feven or eight miles an hour. At its firft appearance you can hardly fuppofe it the fame river, for where the tide has effect, it feldom runs more than four miles an hour; it increafes in rapidity as you advance to Montreal, and oppofite the city it runs almoft ten miles an hour, which renders its navigation extremely difficult, as nothing but a very ftrong and favourable wind, with all the fails full fet, can enable veffels to ftem the current. What with unfavourable winds and light breezes, fhips have been as long in getting up from *Trois Rivieres* to Montreal, as they were on their paffage from England to Quebec.

The rapidity of the current makes crof-fing not only difagreeable, but very dangerous, for unlefs you have a fkilful pilot, the current will carry you a league below

where

where you want to land.   And yet it is
furprizing, how expert the Canadians are
with their wooden canoes ; but the Indians
far exeeed them in working theirs, as their
canoes are of a much lighter conftruction.
Both being much ufed in this country,
I fhall endeavour to defcribe them, that
you may be able to form fome idea of what
they are.

Thofe which the Canadians ufe, are
called wooden ones, being hollowed out of
the red elm, fome of which are fo large, as
to contain twenty perfons.

Thofe which the Indians ufe, are made
of the bark of the birch tree, and diftinguifhed by the name of birch canoes, the
different parts of which they few together
with the inner rind of the bark of the tree,
and daub them over with a pitch, or rather
a bituminous matter, refembling pitch, to
prevent their leaking.   They form the ribs
from

from the boughs of the hickory tree, and are conftructed of different dimenfions, fome being only large enough to contain two perfons, and others thirty.

Thefe canoes are eafily managed by the Indians with their paddles, and with the current go at a prodigious rate, for one fingle ftroke with the paddle will force them twice the length of the canoe againft it.   It was with one of thefe birch canoes that General Carleton, with an Aid-de-Camp, made their efcape through the enemy's fleet, when he quitted Montreal, foi the purpofe of putting Quebec in a better ftate of defence.

Unwilling to lofe the opportunity of fending this by an officer who is going to Quebec, I am obliged to put a period to this letter : and, no doubt, upon the perufal of it, you will eafily difcover the young tra-

I 3   veller.

veller, who is diverted with every thing that prefents itfelf to his view But in hopes that it may afford you half an hour's amufement, I remain,

Yours, &c.

LET-

LETTER   XII.

Montreal, November 26th, 1776.

MY DEAR FRIEND,

BEFORE I defcribe to you this city, let me give you fome account of the ifland on which it ftands, and from whence it derives its name.

This ifland, which meafures, ten leagues in length and about four in breadth, is formed by the river St. Laurence, and in the center of it are two large mountains, which are the firft you meet with on the north fide of St. Laurence, and were called by the firft difcoverers of this province,

I 4   *Monts*

Monts Royaux, which gave name to the ifland, afterwards *Mont Royal*, and at laft, by a variety of corruptions of the language, *Montreal*.

Of all the adjacent countries, there is no place where the climate is reckoned to be fo mild, fo pleafant, and the foil fo fruitful: with all thefe natural bleffings, is it not furprizing to fee it thinly inhabited, and very ill fettled, for except two or three miles round the city, the country is moftly woods, interfperfed with a few fmall plantations.

One thing not a little remarkable is, that this ifland contains a fmaller one of about three miles in length, and two and a half in breadth, formed by two inlets of St. Laurence. This little ifland, which is called the *Ifle de Jefus*, is almoft cleared from woods, and has a fmall church and a few houfes on it, rendering Montreal

treal extremely pleasant; being so situated,
that you cannot go a great length in any
direction, before you come to it; and
surely, after travelling through woods and
swamps, it affords a most pleasing relief.

The summit of the mountains I have
described to you are extremely difficult to
gain; but having once accomplished it,
the delightful prospect that presents itself,
amply compensates for the fatigue and
dangers you encounter, being able to view
the whole island, and several leagues round
it. You can plainly discern the mountains that cross *Lake Champlain*, called the
Green Mountains, which are near 60 miles
distant. It appears generally a vast forest,
there being only three objects to diversify
the scene: the view of the city of Montreal, the river St. Laurence, and the
mountains of *Chamblée*, which are exceedingly beautiful, and the more remarkable, being in a plain level country, and
not

not having a fingle hill for feveral leagues round them; they are confiderably loftier than the mountains on this ifland.

This city forms an oblong fquare, divided by regular, well formed ftreets, and the houfes in general are well built; there are feveral churches, but thofe, as well as many of the houfes have felt the effects of this war.

The city is furrounded by a wall and dry ditch, and at one end there is a citadel. Thefe fortifications were raifed many years paft, as a defence againft the Indians, and fince the war, great improvements have been made to them; but the city is fo fituated, that no works can be raifed to enabled it to ftand a regular fiege, having many rifing grounds, that command it in more places than one.

When

When we gained poffeffion of this province, Montreal was nearly as large as Quebec, but fince that time it has fuffered much by fire; it is greatly to be wondered at, that it has not, one time or other, been totally deftroyed: for in the winter, when the inhabitants go to bed, they make great fires in their ftoves, and leave them burning all night, by which means they are frequently red hot before morning. Imagine how very dangerous they muft have been, when their houfes were conftructed of wood; few of thofe are now remaining, except in the outfkirts of the city, the greateft part of them being built of ftone.

The inhabitants here, as well as thofe of Quebec, having fo many times fuffered by fire, conftruct their buildings in fuch a manner, that they are not only perfectly fecure againft that element, but even againft houfe-breakers, which being a little fingular,

fingular, you will have no objection to my defcribing them.

The houfe confifts of one lofty floor, built with ftone, and the apartments are divided by fuch thick walls, that fhould a fire happen in one of them, it cannot communicate to any other : the top of the houfe being covered with a ftrong arch, if the roof which is over it fhould catch fire, it cannot damage the interior part of the houfe. At Quebec, that city having been fo often befieged, the inhabitants who are now building at that place, make this arch bomb-proof.

Each apartment has a double door, the inner one of wood, and the outer one of iron, which is only fhut when the family retire to reft; the windows have double fhutters of the fame materials, and have not only taken this precaution with the doors that lead out of the houfe, but

added

added an iron one, which is fixed on the infide.

Thefe doors and fhutters are made of plate iron, near half an inch thick, which, perhaps, you will imagine, muft give the houfe a very difagreeable appearance, but it is far otherwife, for being moftly painted green, they afford a pleafing contraft to the whitenefs of the houfe.

This is the bufy time of the merchants belonging to this place, who are now ufing all poffible expedition in fending home their furs, before the winter fets in. The reafon affigned for deferring it till fo late in the feafon, is on account of the traders, fome of whom are but juft arrived from the upper countries, the merchants gene-rally waiting as long as there is a poffibility of their return, and fometimes fo long in expectation of them, as to lofe their mar-kets entirely.

Thefe

Thefe traders, in the courfe of their voyages, are continually encountering hardfhips and difficulties, and their lives are frequently in imminent danger :----- nothing can counterbalance the great perils that await them, but the certainty of acquiring an ample fortune in the courfe of three or four voyages.

They fet out in the fpring of the year, in parties of about twenty or thirty perfons, with perhaps eight or ten large birch canoes ; they have no fixed courfe to take, but fteer that where it is imagined they can meet with a tribe of Indians; keeping moftly upon the upper lakes, fometimes carrying their goods and canoes acrofs rapids, which are parts of the river greatly quickened by the defcents, and over land to a river, up which they will proceed many leagues. If they do not meet with any Indians, it obliges them to return again to the lake, and proceed weftward.

The

The goods they take with them to bar-
ter for fkins, confift chiefly of brandy, tobacco, a fort of duffil blanket, guns, powder and balls, kettles, hatchets and tomahawks, as likewife looking-glaffes, vermillion and various other paints; and
according to any article that an Indian has
a defire or an ufe for, he will give ten times
its value in fkins. They are moft eager
after powder, ball, paint, brandy and tobacco.

Thefe traders traverfe vaft lakes and
rivers with incredible induftry and patience, carrying their goods among nations in the remoteft parts of America.
They are generally abfent from their fa-
milies about three years, before their departure make a will, and fettle all their
affairs, many of them, with their whole
party, having been put to death by the
Indians, either for the ftores they carry
with them, or to revenge the death of fome

of

of their nation, who has been killed by
the burfting of a gun that has been fold
to them, which is frequently the cafe, they
being by no means proof. The Indians
do not wait for thofe traders who fold the
gun, but take their revenge upon the firft
they meet with. Here I muft obferve to
you, that the guns which are fold to the
Indians are fitted up in a very neat manner, to attract the notice of thefe poor
creatures, and frequently, after having been
fired five or fix times, they burft, and the
unfortunate purchafer is either killed, or
lofes an hand or an arm. Thefe traders
are certainly the beft judges, but I cannot
help thinking it both cruel and impolitic.

It having been hinted, that a reward
would be given to him who fhould difcover
a north-weft paffage, or whether the Continent joins to India, two fuppofitions
much credited by the Europeans in general;
feveral of the traders have endeavoured to
find

find which is the true one: as there is every
year fome frefh difcovery made, there remains but little doubt that in fome future
time it will be effected. I believe the fartheft that any of them have yet reached
was a Mr. Henry, who is reported to have
travelled for ten days upon a large plain,
on which grew only a rank-grafs, nearly as
high as a man's breaft, and on this plain he
frequently met with immenfe droves of
buffaloes, and obferved the tracks of feveral
others; that on the eleventh day he came
to a vaft river, which ftopped his progrefs,
as he did not chufe to venture croffing in a
canoe; that the water was quite falt, and
run extremely rapid, from which circumftance he concluded there muft be a north-
weft paffage.

Whether it is fo or not, it is to be hoped
that when this unhappy conteft is ended,
Government may think it a matter worthy
their confideration, and fit out an expedi-

K tion

tion for afcertaining it, as the difcovery would not only be of great importance to England, but to all the world. As we have already made fuch great and wonderful difcoveries in the South Seas, furely this will be deemed of fufficient importance to juftify the expence of fitting out proper perfons from England to inveftigate the fact.

If after fo many fruitlefs attempts, fome one fhould appear, whofe firm mind will rife fuperior to every fenfe of danger, encountering variety of hardfhips, and whofe patience is not exhaufted by their duration; if fuch a one, animated with a hope of glory, which alone teaches men to difregard life, rendering them equal to the greateft undertakings; who, being well informed, fo as to underftand what he fees, and of veracity enough to relate only what he has feen---if fuch a man fhould appear, and no doubt there are many who poffefs

thefe

thefe excellent and extraordinary qualifica-
tions, his refearches will perhaps be crown-
ed with better fuccefs. But, if after fuch
an undertaking, this celebrated paffage
fhould ftill remain concealed, it muft be
concluded, either that it doth not exift, or
is not given to man to difcover.

I add nothing more to this letter, fearful
of lofing its conveyance, therefore remain

Yours, &c.

LET.

LETTER XIII.

Montreal, Nov. 30th, 1776.

MY DEAR FRIEND,

A FEW days ago, I made a vifit to our friend Shlagell of the 21ft regiment, at St. John's, where he is ftationed for the winter. I cannot but fay I was much pleafed with the place, it having all the appearance of a dock-yard, and of being equally as bufy. The fleet that was upon the Lake is repairing, as likewife feveral of the veffels that we took from the Americans; they are laid up in docks, to preferve them from the inclemencies of the winter, and by the enfuing fpring, what with the

fhips

fhips we had before, and thofe we have
fince taken from the Americans, we fhall
have a fleet far fuperior to any they can
poffibly bring on the Lakes.

There are two fchooners here, the *Carle-*
ton and *Maria,* which were built in England upon a conftruction to take into pieces,
in order to be tranfported acrofs a carry-
ing-place of about two miles. After their
failing from England to the mouth of the
rapids, which prevented their proceeding
up to St. John's, rather than lofe the time
of taking them to pieces, and re-conftruct-
ing them, Lieutenant Schank, of the navy,
an ingenious officer, informed General
Carleton, that they might be conveyed
upon a cradle over land to St. John's, entire,
provided there was a good road made for
them. The General acquiefced in this
gentleman's propofal, and the whole army
were employed in making a road. One of
the veffels was near half a mile on it, by

K 3

means

means of cables fixed to windlaſſes every
twenty yards ; but the General perceiving
this mode of conveyance would take up
more time than the other, gave orders to
have the ſchooners taken to pieces and re-
built, which was accompliſhed in as ſhort
a ſpace of time as they had been creeping
that ſmall diſtance upon land.

Our naval force being far inferior to
what the Americans had this ſummer upon
the Lakes, it was deemed neceſſary to en-
creaſe it.   The ſhip-wrights were inſtantly
employed to build a frigate, and the army
in cutting the timber for it, which is now
as complete a veſſel as any in the King's
ſervice.   I am afraid you will think I uſurp
the privilege of a traveller, when I tell you
that this frigate was conſtructed in ſo ſhort
a time, that in eight and twenty days after
her keel was laid ſhe was in action ; and
what was ſtill more wonderful, there were
only ſixteen ſhip-wrights to build her, one
of

of whom was, on the third day, fo badly wounded with an adze, as to be of little fervice.

You may eafily imagine how great muft have been the aftonifhment of the Americans when fhe came upon the Lakes, knowing we had no fuch fhip when they abandoned St John's. Notwithftanding this, they fought their fleet bravely, and our new-built veffel, by the falling of the wind, bore but a partial part of the engagement, the ftrefs laying upon the *Carleton* and *Maria* fchooners, which were both much fhattered. On board the latter was General Carleton, who had a very narrow efcape, a cannon fhot paffing clofe by him as he was giving directions to an officer, and which the General with that coolnefs and intrepidity that fo much diftinguifhes his character, took no notice of, but turning round, gave his orders with as much

K 4

com-

compofure as if he had been in the moft
perfect ftate of fecurity.

This place, which is called the key to
Canada, when the works are compleated,
will be of great ftrength; there are tem-
porary barracks at prefent, both for foldiers and artificers. The old barracks, as
well as the fort the Americans deftroyed
when they abandoned the place, were formerly quite furrounded with woods, but
are now clear for fome diftance round.

In order that you may form a juft idea
of this important place, I have enclofed
you a drawing of it, reprefenting the two
redoubts, with the rope-walk, the fhip on
the ftocks, and the other veffels at anchor
near the fort, and which I have taken from
the block-houfe erected on the oppofite fide
of the river Sorell.

From

From this place I went to the *Iſle au Noix*, which is the advanced poſt of the army, on which the 20th regiment is ſtation- ed. This iſland is about a mile and a half in length, and three quarters of a mile in breadth; it was entirely covered with wood, but at preſent greatly cleared, and before the winter is over, we imagine it will be entirely ſo. Although ſo late in the year, and in this ſevere climate, the regiment ſtationed there is encamped, and likely to continue ſo till after Chriſtmas, as it will be that time before the block-houſes in- tended for them are finiſhed.

Block-houſes not being generally known in England, ſhall be my apology for giving you a deſcription of them. They are con- ſtructed of timbers, placed one on the other, of a ſufficient thickneſs to reſiſt a muſquet ſhot, and large enough to contain from 100 to 120 men; there are two apartments in them, one above the other,

in

the upper of which is a divifion for the officers. In both the lower and upper apartments are two pieces of cannon and four port-holes, for the purpofe of point-ing thefe cannon on any fide of the block-houfe on which it may be attacked; and in cafe an enemy fhould in the night en-deavour to fet fire to the houfe, there are loop-holes, through which the troops on the infide can level their pieces and fire upon the affailants. They are reckoned to be a very ftrong defence, as it has been known that a fmall party of men, in one of thefe block-houfes, have repulfed treble their own number. But that you may more fully comprehend the conftruction of thefe unufual fortifications, I have inclofed a drawing and fection of one of them for your infpection.

The foldiers, not only at the *Ifle au Noix*, but likewife at St. John's, have been very fubject to the fcurvy, not having any other

other than falt provifions, but by drinking plentifully of fpruce beer, they are now all in perfect health, which clearly proves that liquor to be a powerful antifcorbutic. It is fo much known in England, as to need no defcription; the only difference between the fpruce there and here is, that here it is made with the branches of the tree itfelf, and there with the effence.

As the feverity of the weather fhuts up all intercourfe by letters, this is the laft you may expect to receive from me till the froft breaks up. But though I cannot write to you, be affured I fhall continually think of you, and remain, with the greateft efteem and fincerity,

Yours, &c.

L E T-

L E T T E R   XIV.

Montreal, January 18*th*, 1777.

MY DEAR FRIEND,

I DID not expect to have written fo foon, but an opportunity of a flag of truce, which is going by the way of Ticonderoga to New-York, unexpectedly occurring, I am happy to embrace it, efpecially when it is impoffible for me to employ my leifure hours more fatisfactory to myfelf, than in endeavouring to divert you.   I fhall therefore proceed to give you fome account of the winter amufements of this place, and among the principal ones is that of carioling upon the ice, the inhabitants making

making large parties every day for that purpofe; they generally go to *Point aux Trembles*, about three leagues from this city, at which place refides a Dutch woman, who makes moft excellent faufages, and at whofe houfe it is cuftomary to refrefh with thefe and bottled porter. As the north wind generally blows very fharp, you acquire a pretty good appetite, and, for my own part, I enjoyed this *petite repas* in preference to my dinner, very few regimental meffes being conducted with that propriety and decorum which fhould characterize the profeffion, as there are generally among them a fet of ungovernable young men. But to return to my defcription of carioling.

You will no doubt think it too much to go nine miles and back again for a jaunt before dinner; but this mode of travelling is fo very expeditious, that moft of the inhabitants defer their journey to Quebec till

till this feafon of the year, as they can perform it with lefs difficulty, and much greater expedition.

The carioles are fafhioned after different devices, to imitate birds and beafts, but in general they are of one conftruction, with only this difference, that the common people have theirs clofe upon the ice or fnow, while thofe of their fuperiors are raifed upon what are called runners, which elevate them about two feet. They paint them of various fantaftical colors; many of them, as a contraft to this feafon of the year, are colored in imitation of thunder and lightning. It is certainly a very eafy and expeditious method of travelling, for the horfes of the country will go with eafe fifteen miles an hour upon the ice. The inhabitants think nothing of a journey of forty or fifty miles to fee a friend, and returning the fame day.

Not-

Notwithſtanding the river runs ſo rapid
as I have before deſcribed, and is now entirely frozen over, yet there are certain
warm ſprings that never will congeal; to
caution travellers, every pariſh, as ſoon as
the river is frozen over, is obliged to fix
large pine trees in the ice, diſtant from
each other about ten feet, which receiving
moiſture from the ice, and being an ever-
green, continue ſo the whole winter, ſo
that when travelling, it appears as if you
were going between an avenue of firs.

On each ſide of the river it is quite
ſmooth, but in the center, where the current runs ſo rapid, the ice is thrown up in
prodigious hills, through which the inhabitants are obliged to cut a paſſage to croſs
the river; the ſides are frozen ſo as to bear
carriages, long before the center, and when
that freezes, no thunder can equal the
noiſe, the reaſon of which you will eaſily
imagine, for where theſe rapids are, the
ice

ice is thrown up in a continual fucceffion of hills; between thefe hills, you are furrounded with ice feveral yards high, and there it is inconceivably cold; when upon the top of one of thefe hills, you cannot help ftopping to view the many curious forms the ice is thrown into, fome of it being in that of a pyramid, other pieces that of a cone, others again in large flabs, and fome of it refembling the figures of men, birds and beafts; in fhort, no defcription can equal fo romantic a profpect.

The Canadians have a very fingular cuftom among them, at the commencement of the year, the men go round the city and falute the ladies, who fit up in ftate for three days for that purpofe, and as the inhabitants are acquainted with each other, the lady is generally faluted by the greateft part of the men; the falutation is after the French fafhion, upon the cheek, when

having

having faluted one, the lady prefents the other.

The European ladies who are fettled here, rather than appear fingular, adopt this cuftom, only varying the falutation after the Englifh fafhion; not but what I think the French mode preferable on this occafion, where the lady is under the neceffity of receiving the falute of every one. As I know you will make this obfervation, *I dare fay he went his rounds*, let me candidly acknowledge I did, and with another officer. We had a very great mortification in going to the houfe of an Englifh merchant, who has a beautiful wife: upon our entering, we difputed who fhould falute her firft; you may fuppofe how eager we both were in our addreffes upon entering the room, and would have enjoyed our chagrin, when we faw General Phillips there, whofe departure muft be waited for, before we could falute the lady; perhaps you will say the pleasure was heightened by contemplating her charms---*Præstat expectare.*

This being the first Catholic country I ever was in, you must suppose me particularly attentive to their religious ceremonies at Christmas. I had ever conceived, that most authors had greatly exaggerated their accounts upon that head, and had I not met with convincing proofs, my candor could not suppose that mankind were so weak in their understandings. That the lower class of people should be led away is not to be wondered at, but how men of learning, sound sense and good understanding should, is to me astonishing. It is allowable for every man to worship any thing symbolically, but their doing it in reality never can be admitted. ✳These superstitious people implicitly believe, the waxen images that are shewn them by their priests, to be absolutely the persons they are intended to represent.

On

On Chriſtmas Eve, I went to the great church, where there was a prodigious con-courſe of people, and got as near as I could to the altar, to obſerve the ceremonies. About nine o'clock the ſervice began with prayers and anthems, which laſted till ten, when the cradle was brought in, upon which there was a great ſhout; after this they continued ſinging and praying till the clock ſtruck twelve, when the high prieſt brought in a wax figure of a child, ſuperbly dreſſed, the muſic ſtruck up, and there was a ſecond great ſhouting. The child being depoſited in the cradle, it was rocked till about one o'clock, when the ceremony finiſhed.

In ſome of the convents they are ex-ceedingly curious in their wax images: there was a repreſentation of the Meſſiah, which was daily varied in its ſize, from the time of its ſuppoſed birth, till the time the Monks had fixed as neceſſary for its

being

being sufficiently grown to represent our Saviour, at the age he was when he preached in the Temple. When I first went to see this wax-work, on the Christmas-day, there was a figure of Joseph, dressed in a scarlet cloak, with a large tie wig, another to resemble the Virgin Mary with a little child, laying in a manger, and over it was the figure an ox and an afs's head, which are at the same time emblematical of their own stubbornefs and stupidity. In a few days this representation was changed, and there was another of the Wife Men making their offerings to the *Salvator Mundi*; so continuing every remarkable event of his life, till the time of preaching in the Temple; and whenever I went, there was always a vast concourse of people upon their knees praying to these figures. This mode of religion appears to me to be extremely well calculated to inspire devotion in the lower clafs of people, yet it is great pity some better method of paying adoration

tion

tion to the Divine Being cannot be adopted to infpire a true fenfe of his exiftence,
than means fo abfurd.   Difference of
opinion concerning religion ever will prevail, but left you think I am growing too
fermonic, I fhall conclude this fubjeƈt with
an obfervation of a *Monfieur Blondeaux*, at
whofe houfe I am quartered, and who is a
very fenfible and intelligent man.

Converfing with him, one day, on their
worfhipping thefe waxen images, and other
ridiculous ceremonies in their religion,
Monfieur, faid he, *Mon avis eft que chacun
doit fuivre la religion pour laquelle il fe font
plus d'inclination; et je fuis affuré qu'au jour
du jugement, on ne nous demandra pas quelle
religion nous avons profeffée; mais que nous
ferons tous recompenfés on punis felon nos actions.*

As I informed you this goes by a flag of
truce, it would be unpardonable to omit

L 3   men-

humane General

mentioning the humanity of General Carleton, who has cloathed all thofe who were taken prifoners, they being almoft in a ftate of nakednefs; many of them he fuffered to return to their homes upon their paroles of not bearing arms again during the war. Thofe who are here to be exchanged are cloathed, and fare the fame as our own foldiers.

Fate can only determine whether I fhall experience the misfortune of being taken prifoner, but, if I fhould, it is my hope that I may not meet with worfe treatment than thefe people have received.

By the mode this will be conveyed, I am not certain that it may reach you; but if it fhould, it brings you my beft wifhes for your health and happinefs, and an affurance that I am, with great fincerity,

Yours, &c.

LET-

LETTER XV.

Montreal, January 28th, 1777.

MY DEAR FRIEND,

THE winter is now fet in with great feverity, and you would naturally conclude that this country is the moft un- comfortable in the world, and its inhabi- tants the moft unhappy, but far from it: the city and the country people around, feem to be perfectly in their element; there is nothing but carioling, feafting, and other amufements. The Canadians perfectly refemble the French with refpect to dancing, having meetings at each other's houfes for that purpofe almoft every night.

winter a time of games for Canadians instead of complaints

L 4   Though

Though the weather is fo fevere, the inhabitants here never ftay in doors in the
day, unlefs it fnows, which feldom happens, for the firft fall is generally the only
one they have, and that lafts for two or
three days, after which the weather is
fettled, and has been extremely pleafant
for this month paft; excepting one day,
there has been quite an Italian fky, not a
cloud to be feen.

The air of Canada is reckoned the moft
falubrious and healthy of any in the world;
yet notwithftanding this, the Canadians
are very confumptive, and it is incredible
what numbers of them die before they
arrive at maturity; if they furvive that
period, they moftly live to a good old age.

A very eminent phyfician, Dr. Kennedy,
who is with our army, attributes this entirely to the ftoves they make ufe of in the
winter, and that was any other mode of
conveying

conveying warmth fubftituted, they would in all probability be a long lived people. For, fays he, the inhabitants moftly keep their ftoves heated, and in coming out of the frefh air to enter a room where there is one, you are almoft fuffocated. How pernicious this muft be to the conftitution, efpecially of the young children, who are continually going in and out of the heated rooms into the fnow and upon the ice; and when the lungs and pores are expanded by the heat of thefe ftoves, run without any addition of cloathing into the cold, where the blood receives fo fudden a change, that it generally leaves fome fatal diforder upon the lungs.

It is very difficult to eradicate long efta-blifhed prejudices and cuftoms, but if the Canadians were to adopt the mode of other northern climates, where the cold is nearly as intenfe as it is here, I think they would experience the benefits arifing from it.

In

In Ruffia, Germany, and in all the northern parts upon the Continent in Europe, the inhabitants have ftoves fimilar to the Canadians, but fo conftructed, that when the room is of a fufficient warmth, the front opens with two folding doors, where there is a good fire in a grate, and the fulphureous air exhales up the funnel, by which means they enjoy an agreeable warmth; if they perceive it getting cold, they fhut the doors for a little while, till the room is fufficiently heated. The Canadian ftoves are fo conftructed, that the whole time you are in a room, you are almoft ftifled with the fulphureous vapor, which muft be extremely pernicious, and in all probability occafions the fallow complexion of the Canadians; there cannot be a ftronger proof that it is fo, than its having the fame effect on Europeans who have been fettled here any length of time.

They

They put me in mind of Erasmus's *Diversoria Germanica*-----B. *In hypocausto exuis ocreas; induis calceos; mutas, si voles, indusium, vestes pluvia madidas suspendis juxta hypocaustum; ipse te admoves, ut sicceris. Itaque frequenter in idem hypocaustum conveniunt octaginta aut nonaginta, pedites, equites, negotiatores, nautæ, aurigæ, agricolæ, pueri, fæminæ, sani, ægroti.*---Gu. *Istuc verè cænobium est.*---Be. *Alius ibi pectit caput, alius abstergit sudorem, alius repurgat perones aut ocreas, alius eructat alium. Quid multis? Ibi linguarum ac personarum non minor est confusio, quàm olim in turri Babel. Prodit famulus senex barbâ canâ, tonso capite, vultu torvo, sordido vestitu.*---Gu. *Tales opportebat cardinalibus Romanis esse à poculis.*---Be. *Is circumactis oculis tacitus dinumerat, quot sint in hypocausto: quo plures adesse videt, hoc vehementius accenditur hypocaustum etiamsi alioque sol æstu sit molestus. Hæc apud illos præcipua pars est bonæ tractionis, si sudore diffluant omnes. Si quis non assuetus vapori, aperiat rimam*

rimam feneſtræ, nè præfocetur, protinus audit,
Claude. *Si reſpondeas,* Non fero : *audis,*
Quære igitur aliud diverſorium.---Gu. *At-*
que mihi nihil videtur periculoſius, quàm tam
multos haurire eundem vaporem, maximè reſo-
luto corpore, atque hic capere cibum, et horas
complures commorari. Tum enim omitto ructus
alliatos, et ventris flatum, halitus putres :
multi ſunt qui morbis ocultis laborant, nec ullus
morbus non habet ſuum contagium.---Be. *Sunt*
viri fortes, iſta rident ac negligunt.---Gu. *Sed*
interim multorum periculo fortes ſunt.---You
will pardon me ſuch a long quotation, but
it is ſo appoſite, that I could not reſiſt it.

Although the weather is intenſely cold,
the mode of dreſs in uſe here, and theſe
ſtoves, prevent your ever feeling any;
there are none of thoſe raw damp days, ſo
much the ſubject of complaint in England,
and from the bad effects of which no
cloathing will defend you.

The

The drefs of the natives is extremely
well calculated for the climate; it confifts
(in addition to the common habiliments *Canadian drefs*
worn in England) of a blanket coat, a pair
of what are called leggings, with a kind
of flap on the outfide of the leg, to prevent the fnow from clogging round them;
fur gloves, and a fur cap, which is made
to pull over the ears, but this is feldom
done, except when the ftrong north-weft
winds blow. At that time it is very dangerous to go out, as you run a great
rifque of being froft-bit, which happens in
an inftant, fometimes in turning the corner of a ftreet, without being fenfible of it
at the time, as it occafions no fort of pain;
if the part affected is not immediately
rubbed with fnow, and every precaution
taken, it is fure to mortify, and fhould any
one, thus circumftanced, be imprudent
enough to go near the fire, mortification is
inevitable.

To

To convince you how very inftantaneous it muft be, I fhall relate a ludicrous cir-cumftance, which however had nearly been productive of a duel.

An officer in the garrifon having a nofe remarkably large, was going to dinner at the mefs, when not four doors from his lodgings, turning round a corner, he met another officer, who immediately cried out, " God blefs me, your nofe is froft-bit." From the fmall diftance he had gone, he thought it impoffible, and that his friend was bantering him ; high words arofe, and they parted with an appointment to meet the next morning, to refent the affront. He made hafte to his dinner, and upon his entering the room, the officers prevented his coming to the fire, telling him at the fame time his nofe was froft-bit. He then began to think it no joke, and was happy to apply the ufual remedy : it was no bad punifhment for his rafhnefs and incredu-lity,

lity, that during the time the officers were at dinner, he was obliged to be in the cold, rubbing his nofe with fnow till the blood circulated, and though very fharp fet, obliged to nofe a meal he would have been happy to partake of.

The prefent feafon of the year not per- mitting any military manœuvres, and na- turally inclining us more to reflections of a ferious nature, than the gay appearance of the fpring or fummer, I fhall again trefpafs on your patience with fome few obfervations on the effects of the intenfe cold weather experienced in this country; and as you have always appeared partial to my adding the remarks of others, where I thought them more juft and beautiful than my own, I fhall allude to fome that ftruck me on the following phœnomena.

I have already mentioned to you that the froft is fet in, and among the many incon- veniencies

veniencies which the inhabitants of this
northern region fuffer from it, none is
more to be lamented than that of the
ground being fo much frozen, as to make
it impoffible to dig a grave for the inter-
ment of thofe who die at this time; their
friends are obliged to keep them above
ground till a thaw comes, when they return the body to the duft from whence it
came.

[handwritten margin note: in winter impoffible to dig graves — so that dead muft wait until spring to be buried.]

You will eafily conceive, my dear friend,
that the daily fight of fo mournful an object as the bier of a departed hufband, muft
inevitably lengthen out the forrow of

> " The new made Widow—
> Whilft bufy meddling Memory,
> In barbarous fucceffion, mufters up
> The paft endearments of their fofter hours,
> Tenacious of its theme."

To relatives, who often think it a religious duty to mourn the departed, fuch
fcenes,

ſcenes, by a protracted ſorrow, often draw life to its utmoſt verge, and at the funeral they are ſcarce more alive than the corpſe they bury. To thoſe who, without feeling a loſs, are yet led to contemplate, it often ſuggeſts the idea of Arbuthnot,

" What am I ? how produc'd ? and for what end ?
Whence drew I being ? to what period tend ?

I think you would hardly forgive me, were I not to relate to you the very ſtrange manner in which theſe thoughts affect the German ſoldiers of our army. I know not whether to call it ſympathy, or by any other name, but it ſtrongly evinces the connexion exiſting between the body and mind.

how this affects the Germans

The Germans, to the number of twenty or thirty at a time, will in their converſations relate to each other, that they are ſure they ſhall not live to ſee home again, and are

Vol. I.   M   certain

certain that they shall very soon die : would you believe it, after this they mope and pine about, haunted with the idea, that

German soldiers fear they will die, they mope for days

> " Nor wives, nor children, shall they more behold,
> Nor friends, nor sacred home."

Nor can any medicine or advice you can give them divert this settled superstition, which they as surely die martyrs to, as ever it infects them.   Thus it is that men, who have faced the dangers of battle and of shipwreck without fear (for they are certainly as brave as any soldiers in the world), are taken off, a score at a time, by a mere phantom of their own brain.   This is a circumstance well known to every one in the army.

Thus some die probably due to the thought of death alone

In case of any decease in the family of a Canadian, the corpse is deposited in some private chamber, but in our general hospital there is a long room appropriated for
that

that purpofe. The fuperintendant of this room, an apothecary, being a man poffeffed of whimfical ideas, and a turn for the ludicrous, had placed the dead bodies of thefe poor Germans in various poftures, fome kneeling with books in their hands, others fitting down with pipes in their mouths, many ftanding erect againft the wall, and as they have their cloaths on, you fcarcely at firft imagine they are dead; but upon a nearer approach, what with their long muftaches, which are put in form, and their ghaftly countenance, you cannot picture to yourfelf any thing fo horrible, yet at the fame time fo truly laughable and ridiculous.

After what I have related, you will moft probably agree with me, that the conftitution of England has not unwifely declared apothecaries and furgeons incapable of compofing a jury upon trials for capital

M 2 offences

offences, though it excludes fome few of
them who do honor to the profeffion, by
their gentlenefs and humanity: yet I am
fearful the major part of them would not
join in the warmth that is fo frequently
experienced, in the generous and noble
burfts of joy that overwhelms the order of
our courts of juftice, when unprotected
innocence efcapes the arbitrary and re-
vengeful profecution of malice and power.
I have heard furgeons, as an excufe for
the ftrange want of feeling either brought
on by the daily vifitation of ficknefs and
pain, or which they poffefs from the
apathy of their nature, fay, that were
they to feel much on the occafion, it would
difable them from doing their duty. Strange
argument this! and as contradictory to
found fenfe as true philofophy, which might
teach them gentlenefs in the manner, and
firmnefs in the execution. For my own
part, fuch is the fituation of my mind,
when I am indifpofed, that I have fancied
the

the affectionate " how do ye" of the furgeon and apothecary, has done me as much
good as their drugs, or the performance
of an operation in phlebotomy. Can any
one conceive it proper, when a youth of
fixteen has broke a leg, that the furgeon,
while in doubt on the firft vifit, fhould, in
the prefence of his patient, refufe to fearch
whether a fracture had actually happened,
becaufe *he would make fuch a roaring and a*
noife that he fhould not get it out of his head
for a fortnight, and though the lad with
fpirit affured him, that thofe who were
prefent had not feen him fhed a tear; the
furgeon, however, did not make the expe-
riment, though I believe for a much better
reafon than he gave, which was that the
leg was much fwelled. Thus did a furgeon,
while I was in England, treat our coufin
B---, lowering his fpirits, leaving him three
or four days in fufpence, whether his leg
was broken or not, merely to fhew how

M 3   coolly

coolly he could talk on a fubject like that
before him. Had he, inftead of this un-
feeling excufe, but tenderly affured his
patient, that it would put him to more
pain to make the fearch then, than at a
future time, I fhould have fuppofed it
would have made his mind more eafy, and
been the means of preventing the accefs of
a fever, always to be feared on thefe occafions.

In the hofpitals, perhaps the multipli-
city of cafes may plead an excufe for little
ceremony, but in private practice, where
they are well paid, thus wantonly to wound
the feelings of thofe who are but in ill
fpirits, cannot add either to their credit or
practice.

You will long ere this wonder how I
have ftrayed from the wild fcenes that fur-
round me, to lafh the hardened profeffors
of

of the Efculapian art, but you too well know that fuch things do exift, not to pardon my deviation. I fhall therefore conclude with my fincere wifhes that you may never have the misfortune to fall into their hands, and remain

Yours, &c

LET-

L E T T E R XVI.

Montreal, February 27th, 1777.

MY DEAR FRIEND,

AS my laſt was liable to the infpection of the enemy, I been have reſtrained from informing you of many things that it would otherwiſe have communicated. I embrace, therefore, the opportunity of an officer going to Quebec, in order that you may receive this by the firſt ſhip that ſails for England.

Since my laſt I have been again to St. John's, where, notwithſtanding the ſeverity of the weather, the artificers and ſhip-wrights

wrights are all bufily employed. We have raifed upon the Lakes, in addition to the force of laft fummer, a curious veffel, called a *Radeaux*, which formerly belonged to the French, and was funk by the Americans near this place : it is a caftle of itfelf, of a monftrous conftructure, and will hold a great number of men; fhe is intended to convey the heavy artillery acrofs the Lakes. From the account, indeed, that we have received from fome deferters, the Americans do not intend to difpute them, but wait our arrival at Ticonderoga.

The garrifon at St. John's has been kept very alert moft of the winter, as feveral parties of the enemy have come acrofs the Lake upon fleighs, and having hovered about the woods, twice attacked the blockhoufe on the oppofite fhore, their views, no doubt, were of deftroying our fleet; but to render the fhips more fecure, the ice has been cut away for feveral yards round

round them, to prevent their being fet
fire to.

As I returned from St. John's along the
river, my attention was fuddenly caught
by an object well calculated to have exer-
cifed the feelings, and employed the pen of
a Sterne.

When the river freezes over, the Canadians cut a fquare hole in the ice, for the
cattle to drink out of. I faw a drove of
fheep furrounding one of thefe holes: the
whole flock looked moft piteoufly, and
bleated with fo mournful a lamentation,
as would have pierced a heart of ftone; one
of them feemed infinitely more agitated
than the reft, and exhibited feelings that
would have done honor to the moft tender
fenfibility.   Curiofity, concern, or what
you will, led me inftantly to the mouth of
the hole, where a poor little lamb, not four
days old, urged by extreme thirft, had
fallen

fallen in; it was ſtruggling for life, and
ſent forth ſuch diſtreſsful cries!---my God,
how my pulſe beat, and my breaſt was full,
even to burſting!---how often did it get its
little feet on flakes that ſeemed to promiſe
it ſupport, and as often it ſlipt back again
into the water; now it ſeemed by ineffectual exertions, anxious for life, and now
hopeleſs and deſpairing, lay inanimate;---
it was ſome time before I could extricate it;
do me juſtice, and gueſs my feelings till I
had effectually ſaved its life. I took it up
in my arms, and the whole flock followed
me to the farm houſe. To deſcribe the
mother's ſolicitude, and the joy at finding
it ſafe, is impoſſible; language can never
betray what the imagination itſelf can
ſcarcely paint. You who are poſſeſſed of
ſympathy, and a tender regard for the whole
creation, which is perhaps the greateſt ornament of human nature, will eaſily believe
the infinite pleaſure this little office of humanity afforded me.

This

This is one of the many things in which the mind might be apt to arraign the wifdom of Providence, why nature fhould give birth to fuch tender creatures, at fo rigorous a feafon of the year, when to all appearance they require the utmoft warmth to bring them to perfection.

A few days fince I went to *Verchere*, to fee fome officers of the 24th regiment, which village is extremely pleafant, commanding a very extenfive view both ways of the river, with a profpect of this city. It derives its name from a circumftance, wherein it is proved that the fair fex, upon emergencies, poffefs a courage equal, if not fuperior to ours. In the year 1690, when this province was in a continual ftate of warfare with the Indians, and the inhabitants were obliged to refide in forts, it happened that a *Madame de Verchere* was left alone in the fort, whilft the reft of the people were at work in the fields; a fmall

party

party of Indians gaining this intelligence, were determined to enter the fort, plunder it, and take her prifoner; *Madame de Ver-chere*, however, perceiving them approach in a pofture for fcaling the palifado, fired fome mufquet fhot, and drove them to a diftance; they inftantly returned, and were again repulfed, aftonifhed, you may be fure, fince they could only difcover a woman, who appeared as undifmayed as if fhe had been furrounded with a nume-rous garrifon. The Indians knowing the place was unprovided with any other de-fence, made feveral attempts, and were always repulfed by the lady, who defended herfelf in the fort for near four hours, with a valor and prefence of mind which would have done honor to an old warrior: they were at length compelled to retire entirely, as the inhabitants of the fort (who always went out to labor with their mufquets, in cafe of an attack) were returning, and greatly fuperior in number to the Indians. This

was

was not the only inftance of this lady's
courage, for about two years after, a party
of the fame Indians, but much more numerous, furprized and took prifoners the
men, when at work; a little girl happened
to make her efcape, who, running into
the fort acquainted *Madame de Verchere*
of what had happened. Shortly after the
Indians appeared before the fort, leading
the men captive. There was not a foul
left in it, befides a young foldier and a
number of women, who raifed moft lament-
able cries at the fight of their hufbands
being led prifoners. In the midft of this,
Madame de Verchere loft neither her courage
nor prefence of mind, for after locking up
the women, that their groans and weeping
might not infpire the Indians with additional courage, and affuming the habiliments of a foldier, fhe fired a piece of cannon and feveral mufquet fhot, fhewing herfelf with her foldier, fometimes in one redoubt and fometimes in another, always
firing

firing upon the approach of the Indians to the breaſt-work, who did not make a fierce aſſault, as by her ſtratagem they ſuppoſed there were many men in the garriſon. Fortunately for the lady, ſhe had not long to remain in this diſagreeable ſtate, for the *Chevalier de Criſaſy* who was Governor of a ſmall fort at *Chamblée*, upon hearing the firing of cannon, came to the ſuccour of the place, and that ſo ſuddenly, that the Indians were obliged to make a very precipitate retreat, leaving their priſoners behind them.

This remarkable lady lived to a good old age, and died in Normandy, where there is a monument erected to her, with theſe two ſingular inſtances of her fortitude and bravery.

One would imagine that this ſpot of *Verchere* was deſtined for the trial of fortitude and bravery in the fair ſex, to which I

might

First mention
Madame
Reidsarhel

might add conjugal affection. At this time a lady refides here, noble by birth, in whom is united all the foftnefs and delicacy of her fex, ever accuftomed to thofe elegancies and refined enjoyments which are attendant upon high rank and fortune: fhe has forfaken all the pleafures of the gay and fafhionable world, to accompany her hufband to the wild forefts of Canada; already travelled a vaft extent of country, in different extremities of feafon, and with difficulties that an European will not eafily conceive. Such inftances of connubial attachment, in the levity of the prefent day, are rarely to be met with; but that fuch characters do exift, and that the pleafures and gaieties of the *beau monde* have not altogether vanquifhed the focial virtues, is to be inftanced in that pattern of her fex, Lady Harriet Ackland, who has not only encountered the hardfhips already defcribed, but upon joining the army, in addition to her former fatigues, had to attend her hufband upon

upon his fick bed, in a miferable hut at *Chamblée*. A mind like hers, animated by love and affection, is alone capable of encountering fuch hardfhips.

General Phillips commands this garrifon, and is much efteemed by the officers of the army ; he gives them as little trouble as poffible, but will have them perform their duty, and feldom miffes coming upon the parade in a morning. The following anecdote will give you a trait of his character, and fhew you the method he has of gaining the efteem of the officers :

One evening feveral young officers of the artillery having made a little too free with " the Tufcan grape, and being high in blood," went to the houfe of a Canadian, the father of three very pretty daughters : it happened the young ladies were at home, and as they had frequently given fome little encouragement to the officers, thefe young

Vol. I.   N   men

men thought themfelves warranted in taking a few liberties with them; but, as the
wine had deprived them of all ideas of reftraint, they proceeded farther than the
rules of decency or delicacy allow of, or
than I chufe to relate.   In the midft of this
fcene the father arrived, whofe appearance
added greatly to the confufion, and the old
gentleman making a general alarm and
outcry, the officers were obliged to de-
camp.

The next morning a formal complaint
was made to General Phillips, by the father
of the young ladies, who faid that if he
was not immediately redreffed, he would
fet off for Quebec, and lay his complaint
before General Carleton, at the fame time
informing him who had been the aggreffors,
adding, with fome warmth, *Qu'il étoit bien
certain que ce bon General lui rendroit juftice.*

The

The General profeſſed himſelf extremely ſorry that ſuch a diſgrace ſhould have fallen upon the officers of that garriſon, and that he ſhould, for his own ſake, render him all the juſtice in his power, in order to wipe off ſuch a ſtigma from his own corps, which pacified the Canadian.

The next day being the General's levee, thoſe officers, who were now become conſcious of their imprudent behaviour, did not abſent themſelves, leaſt it ſhould argue guilt. After the General had made his bow of retirement to the levee, he deſired that the officers of the artillery would remain, and the reſt of the company being departed, he addreſſed them in the following manner:

" Gentlemen, I have had a very heavy
" complaint made to me by one of the in-
" habitants, of ſome of the officers of the
" artillery, and cannot but ſay I feel it

N 2 " more

" more forcibly, as commanding that corps
" ---and of such a nature too---Gallantry
" has ever marked the soldier's character,
" and I could allow you to use every per-
" suasive argument that lays in your power,
" but for Heaven's sake, don't use violence,
" that is beneath a man!---For my own
" part, I do not know who has been guilty
" of such conduct, nor can I form the
" least idea of the person, unless it was
" Capt. H---, (pointing to an old and in-
" firm officer) I am sure it could not be
" any of the young gentlemen, certainly
" their persons and address would have
" ensured them success. When you solicit
" the fair, violence becomes unnecessary.
" I neither know who the officers were,
" nor do I wish to be informed; but let
" me advise them to pursue different means,
" when they next address the ladies, as
" they may rest. assured those they have
" adopted will never succeed. I only desire
" that I may never hear of any more such

com-

" complaints, nor need I fuggeft to thofe
" gentlemen who are confcious of having
" been concerned in this affair, that it is
" compatible with their characters, to
" make every fatisfaction and apology for
" their conduct, to the father of the young
" ladies."

I need not obferve, that thofe who had
been the caufe of this handfome reprimand
of the General's, immediately went and
made the required apology. Thus, by
the natural politenefs and addrefs of General Phillips, ended a bufinefs, which,
under the cognizance of a more auftere
commander, might have been rendered
fatal to the characters and fortunes of thofe
who had erred only in the moment of ine-
briation.

Moft of the inhabitants have large holes
dug in their cellars, which they fill with
ice, and thofe who have them are now
laying

laying it in for the fummer. I am informed the heat is equally as predominant as the cold is at prefent, and were it not for the ice cellars, they could not keep their provifions fweet a day. At this feafon of the year, the inhabitants have very little trouble in going to market, having only the article of eggs and butter to purchafe, for as foon as the froft fets in, they generally purchafe what provifions they think will ferve them till it breaks up, not only flefh and fowl, but even fifh, for they make holes in the ice, and let down nets five or fix fathom long, which feldom are drawn up empty, and thefe articles, when brought for fale, are frozen as hard as a ftone; the provifions being laid in fo long before they have occafion to ufe them, are always tender. When they want to drefs any thing, it is put into a pail of cold water before the fire, otherwife the water would foon be congealed; in about an hour,

hour, whatever kind of provifion is put in thaws, and becomes fit for ufe.

The lower clafs of Canadians are exceedingly infolent, and infult the officers upon every occafion; their behaviour would be infufferable, did they not now and then get feverely chaftifed. Was I induced to hazard an opinion as to the caufe of this, I fhould attribute it to the very great indulgence fhewn to them by General Carleton; they imagine it is only to lay their complaints, however abfurd, before him, and be redreffed, according to the ftory they tell him. The following is the beft fpecimen I can give you, in confirmation of my affertion :

As Colonel Carleton was driving his cariole, with a lady in it, upon the ice, a Canadian drove his fleigh defignedly againft the Colonel's cariole, by which it was overfet and much damaged : upon this the

N 4   Colonel

Colonel gave him a moſt ſevere horſe-
whipping, which the Canadian bore very
patiently, ſaying, with a ſlight ſhrug,
*Fouëttez donc Monſieur, juſques a ce que vous
ſoyez fatigué, mais je vous aſſure je me'n
plaindrai au General Carleton.* The Colonel then encreaſed his flagellation, telling
him at the ſame time, *Et quand vous vous
plaindrez au Général, ayez la bonté de l'in-
former en même tems, que c'eſt ſon frère qui
vous a fouëtté.* The Canadian hearing this,
and preſuming he ſhould then obtain no
redreſs, began to aſk pardon, became very
ſubmiſſive, and was glad to make the beſt of
his eſcape, by ſlinking away and drawling
out, *Que ſi'l eut ſu que c'etoit le frère du bon
Général, il n'auroit pas fait cela pour tout
au monde.*

This little anecdote, while it convinces
you what great lengths theſe plebeians go,
when they imagine themſelves protected,
will afford you an example of that mean-
neſs

nefs ever attendant upon vulgar and bafe minds, when a proper chaftifement is beftowed upon them, for fuch inftances of their audacity.

I am juft informed there is an opportunity of fending letters to Quebec, from whence this will foon reach you, with my fincere wifhes for your health and happinefs. I remain,

Yours, &c.

LET-

LETTER XVII.

Montreal, April 6th, 1777.

MY DEAR FRIEND,

AS we are now in daily hopes of the froſt's breaking up, and every one is anxious and impatient to hear from his friends, do not let me meet with a diſappointment.

Being deſirous to viſit every place worthy of notice, I went to *Chamblée*, where are the remains of a fort, formerly built by by the French, for what purpoſe they are the beſt judges : it is ſaid their intention was to prevent an army entering Canada.

It

It is fo fituated, that an army can march by *La Prairé* and *La Chine*, take *Montreal*, and then turn their whole force againft the fort, which would be thus cut off from any relief. This has been clearly evinced this war, when General Prefcott, with fe-veral companies, were taken prifoners in it.

The fort is built of ftone, of a regular fquare, with four baftions at each angle, without any out-works, and is fituated a few miles from the mountains which I have already defcribed ; from its fituation I can never fuppofe it otherwife than intended as a magazine for ftores and provifions to fupply St. John's.

About three miles from the fort are the rapids, which prevent fhipping going up to St. John's ; there is a faw-mill there, and it being the firft of the kind I ever faw, I was particular in my examination of it.

After

After the owner had given me every neceffary information, I afked him which Government he preferred, when he exclaimed,
*Oh! Monfieur, il n'y a point de comparaifon,
l'Anglois l'Anglois!* and then related a circumftance, which no doubt you will fay
carried a powerful reafon for the poor old
man's giving us the preference, and affords
another proof how much the Canadians
were opprefled by the French.

There was a cuftom, which is continued
for the repair of roads, tranfporting provifions, and other fervices for Government,
called a *corvée;* it is in the breaft of the
Captains of the Militia to nominate fuch
a number of inhabitants to go with horfes
and carts upon that duty.

At the time Lord Amherft was expected
to enter Canada, acrofs Lake *Champlain,*
the French were continually fending fupplies of ammunition and provifions to
                                    Cham-

Chamblée and St. John's, and the inhabitants, as well as their cattle, were almost worked and harraffed to death, by the oppreffion and tyranny of the Captains of Militia.

Before the campaign commenced, General Montcalm went to St. John's and *Chamblée*, to fee that thofe garrifons were in a perfect ftate of defence, when the poor peafants affembled in a body round him, and fell on their knees to tell their grievances. The man who owned the fawmill told the General he was willing to ferve *le Grand Monarque*, but he had been much oppreffed; that his harveft and plantation had been neglected, and his family almoft ruined and ftarving; and, to add to his misfortunes, *que le deux feuls chevaux qui lui refioient étoient morts de fatigue la veille*: to which the General, inftead of comforting and redreffing the poor old man, with a very ftern look, and at the fame time

time twirling his *croix de St. Louis*, replied, *Mais vous en avez les peaux, c'eſt beaucoup, c'eſt beaucoup!*

Among the various amuſements we enjoyed while away this long winter, I forgot to mention that ſkating is one, which thoſe who are fond of that diverſion are amply indulged in, there being ſuch a conſtancy and large extent of ice. There are ſeveral officers in the regiment, who being exceeding fond of it, have inſtituted a ſkating club, to promote diverſion and conviviality.

The Canadians ſkate in the manner of the Dutch, and exceedingly faſt, but the Indians dart along like lightning. Some years ſince, for a conſiderable wager, three Indians ſet off from this place at day light, and before dark arrived at Quebec, which is 60 leagues; their fatigue, however, was ſo great, that two expired ſhortly after their

their arrival, and the third did not furvive above a week.

In this country there is no fpring nor autumn, and as the froft is daily expected to break, the troops are kept in continual exercife. General Carleton is come to re-view the different regiments; but the fnow is fo deep upon the ground, they are exer-cifed and to be reviewed on the ice, which you would naturally think extremely dan-gerous, and that the men would flip and do one another mifchief with their bayo-nets; but fuch is the power of the fun at this time, that during the day it thaws the furface, which freezing again at night, forms a kind of fmall ice, affording a fteady footing, added to which, all the ice oppofite the city is covered with loofe ftraws blown from the dung. The foil being fo extremely prolific, they have no occafion for manure, and therefore bring

it

it in fleighs upon the ice, to be carried away when it breaks up.

There are many unpleafant duties attending an officer, but none more fo than fitting upon a court-martial.   A few days ago, being upon that duty, I felt myfelf much diftreffed, as being the junior officer, and of courfe the firft to pafs fentence, but was foon releafed from that painful tafk, the culprit efcaping a punifhment, by his blunt oddity.   The crime for which he was tried, and for which he had been twice punifhed before, was that of drunkennefs and diforderly behaviour, which being upon this occafion clearly proved, he was afked by the Prefident what he had to fay in his defence.   He replied, " Oh ! and plaife " your Honors, I have nothing to fay, but " to fave your Honors and the Court any " further trouble, you may fet me down two " hundred, I'm fure your Honors will think " that enough."   The droll and fimple man-

ner

ner in which the fellow fpoke, accompanied
with his dialect, occafioned a fmile upon
every one prefent. After he was ordered
to withdraw, the Court were of opinion,
that as the man was in other refpects a
good foldier, his whimfical manner fhould
in this inftance fave him a punifhment;
when, being called in, and receiving a
fevere reprimand from the Prefident, and
his promifing never to be guilty of the like
again, he was difmiffed. After thanking
the Court for their lenity, he faid, " Since
" as your Honors have been fo good to me,
" I'll *keg* myfelf for fix months, directly I
" get home." As you will not eafily comprehend the word *keg*, or how it can be applied in this inftance, I will explain it to
you : it is a cant word that the foldiers
have among them, when they wifh to refrain from liquors, they take an oath
that for fuch a limited time they will
not touch any fpirits whatever, and if they
are ftrongly addicted to liquor, not hingcan

VOL. I. O tempt

tempt them to tafte any. Perhaps you will fay, it would not be amifs if the officers fometimes followed their example.

It is incredible to think what a difference a few days makes at this feafon of the year. About fix days after our regiment was reviewed, the fnow began to thaw, and is now totally diffolved, except where there has been great drifts, and the ice along the banks has fuch great chafms, that the river is now unfafe to pafs over. The center, where the rapids had thrown up the ice, every now and then breaks, with a noife equal to thunder.

It is aftonifhing how quick vegetation is in this country, you can almoft perceive the grafs grow; the fnow has not been gone many days, and the fields are entirely green, which can only be attributed to the ground's being continually covered with fnow, which nourifhes and preferves
the

the blades with fuch a warmth, that when the fun, which even now is extremely powerful, can come at it, it brings it forward fo very rapidly.

The roads are almoft impaffable, but I am informed that in the courfe of a fortnight they will be as dry and dufty as in the midft of fummer.

In going out of the city towards *Point aux Trembles*, on the right hand, ftand as ftately old houfe, which was built by a perfon, who, after many difappointments and loffes in trade, with the moft unremiting and indefatigable induftry, had fcraped together a plentiful fortune, and as an allufion to the particulars of his life, had carved over his front door the figure of a dog gnawing a large flefhy bone, with this whimfical infcription:

Je fuis le chien qui ronge l'os
Sans en perdre un feul morceau:
Le temps viendra, qui n'eft pas venu
Je mordrai celui, m'aura mordu.

The

The great diverfion of carioling is now over, and the inhabitants are getting ready their calafhes, for they are equally as fond of driving in them as in their carioles.

I am told there is feldom a winter paffes, but feveral people lofe their lives, both before the river freezes over and when the ice breaks up, by being too adventurous in crofling it, a fhocking inftance of which happened three days ago.

Acrofs the chafms made by the ice in breaking up, which fometimes are five or fix yards wide, a bridge of planks is thrown; a cariole paffing over one of thefe, in which was two perfons, the horfe proving unruly, drew it over the fide, and they fell down the chafm near forty feet, where they remained a little time, it being narrow at the bottom, and though every affiftance was inftantly had, no relief could be afforded, as before the ladders and ropes

could

could be let down to them, the weight of the horfe and cariole broke the ice at the bottom, and they were all carried away by the current.

I could not help thinking of the poor lamb in the fame fituation, and lamented the ftriking difference between the defpair of a whole anxious flock for the lofs of a young one, and that buftling coldnefs which difgraced humanity, at the fudden and unexpected death of a man.

The cloathing for the army not being fent out laft year, and as it will be too late to fit it to the men when it arrives, the commanding officers of the different regiments have received orders to reduce the men's coats into jackets, and their hats into caps, as it will be the means of repairing their prefent cloathing, and be more convenient for wood fervice, that when the army take the field, they will in a man-

O 3 ner

ner be all light infantry. The regiments
have the hair that is affixed to their caps
of different colors; ours is red, and as the
pureſt white hair takes the beſt color, ſeveral ſoldiers, ambitious to have theirs ſuperior to the reſt, occaſioned a very ludicrous
affray betwixt them and the inhabitants,
in which the ſoldiers were worſted, and got
a ſevere beating.

They went into a field, to the number of about twenty, and began to cut
the hair from the bottom of the cows
tails : the owner obſerving this, aſſembled
his neighbours and fell upon the ſoldiers
with ſticks, when a ſcuffle enſued, and
the ſoldiers returned home with broken
heads.

Two that had been ſeverely beaten,
made a complaint to the Major of the
regiment, who aſked them if they had on
their ſide-arms, when replying in the negative,

gative, he told them how glad he was they had got a beating; that they fhould always be worn, being the fame to a foldier as a fword was to an officer.

The inhabitants fay, that the winter has been quite mild to what the laft was, and if fo, their hard winters muft be terribly cold; that in general the froft feldom breaks till the end of this month, and fometimes May; and as a proof of its mildnefs, feveral nations of Indians have come fome hundred miles to join the army.

It is a pity their affiftance cannot be difpenfed with, as they will not be reftrained; they are abfolutely neceffary in this woody country, and efpecially as the enemy have them, they are a reftraint upon each other, and I really believe fo much mifchief will not enfue, as if only one party had engaged them. Thofe on our

fide

fide will be fuperior in numbers to the
Americans, as they cannot furnifh them
with neceffary fupplies.

The attachment of the Indian lafts no
longer than you heap prefents on him,
and he fides with that party which will
make the greateft.

Indians go with the greateft awards

It is abfolutely neceffary to keep well
with them, for though there is fuch an
amazing tract of country in poffeffion of
Europeans, it is nothing when put in
competition with the unknown tract that
extends to the weftward. And though
the Indians are much depopulated, ftill
they are a very numerous race of people;
it is altogether unknown where many nations are fettled, nor could it be afcertained any fuch exifted, were it not for
ftraggling Indians belonging to them, that
are cafually met with.

Neceffary to maintain friendfhip wt Indians

Thefe

Thefe people are under great fubjection to their chiefs, and pay implicit obedience to them: They come every year to Montreal, to what is called the fair, when feveral hundreds of them affemble, and are exceedingly troublefome to the inhabitants, they receive prefents to keep them peaceable, and in league of friendfhip; it is incredible what immenfe fums it annually cofts Government for that purpofe.

General Carleton returns to-morrow to Quebec, and as I fend this by one of his Aid-de-Camps, who is going to England, and who has fent his fervant for my letters, I am obliged to conclude haftily, with affuring you, that you fhall hear from me by every opportunity, and remain,

Yours, &c.

LET-

L E T T E R   XVIII.

Montreal, May 20th, 1777.

MY DEAR FRIEND,

NOT having had a letter from you thefe fix months, it is impoffible to exprefs the pleafure yours gave me. I fincerely rejoice that your health is re-eftablifhed, and hope it will always continue fo.

You hint in yours, that great events are expected in the courfe of the enfuing campaign, and that the operations of the two armies will nearly terminate this unfortunate conteft. As to our army, I can only fay,

fay, if good difcipline, joined to health and great fpirit amongft the men, with their being led on by General Burgoyne, who is univerfally efteemed and refpected, can enfure fuccefs, it may be expected ; but, as I obferved before, we have more dangerous enemies at home, than any we have to encounter abroad, for all tranfactions that are to take place are publicly known, long before they are officially given out in orders, and I make no doubt but you will be as much furprized as the General was, when I tell you that the whole operations of the enfuing campaign were canvaffed for feveral days before he arrived, who no doubt. fuppofed, that in giving out his orders he was communicating an entire fecret.

If, therefore, there are people in office, fo imprudent as to communicate any public intelligence, no doubt the numerous agents and well-wifhers to the Americans will

will not be negligent in gaining continual and immediate information. As intelligence is the main fpring of every movement in an army, the Americans will have a great advantage, and what will add conf derably to that advantage, is the great fecrecy they obferve, and the utter impoffibility to obtain the leaft intelligence of any of their defigns, while they are previoufly acquainted with every one of ours.

About three weeks ago the river broke up, which was accompanied with a moft aftonifhing noife : it happened in the night, and you muft judge how ftrange it muft appear, after being ufed to fee, for fuch a length of time, fo fpacious a body of ice, with horfes, carriages, and men travelling on it, changed to a beautiful river, with a number of fhips and boats failing and rowing upon it.

The

The country wears quite a new face, and summer is come all at once. The inhabitants are now bufily employed on their farms, and every thing appears a fcene of buftle and induftry, after fuch a length of time pafied in dull inactivity.

The army is now in movement to take the field; the advanced corps are already encamped at *Boucherville*, and were reviewed by General Burgoyne a few days fince. I accompanied feveral officers to fee them, who had never feen 1500 military men aflembled together.   As to the battalions of the light infantry and grenadiers, fuch a body of men could not be raifed in a twelvemonth, fearch England through. The line of the advanced corps extended a mile; they performed, exclufive of the common manœuvres, feveral new ones, calculated for defence in this woody country, and the General was pleafed to exprefs his approbation in the warmeft terms,

with

with regard to the high difcipline of the men. They proceed in a few days to St. John's, and from thence they are to go upon the Lake, as far as the river *La Cole*, where they are to encamp, till the main body of the army is put in motion.

I was much pleafed at a little politeffe and attention of that amiable woman, Lady Harriet Ackland---Exclufive of the excellent qualities that had already endeared her to the officers of the grenadiers (which corps Major Ackland commands) fhe thought proper to exprefs a fenfe of their attention to her (and who could be inattentive?) by fome little prefent; fo a few days before the officers took the field, fhe fent each of them, (thirty in number) half of a large Chefhire cheefe, which was no fuch fmall prefent as you may imagine, Englifh cheefe being then a dollar per pound; and perhaps it may not occur to you, there is no prefent you can fend to an

European

European abroad, ſo great as good Cheſhire cheeſe. If you ſhould be inclined to ſend me one, and this is no ſmall hint, let me deſire you to encloſe it in lead, and then in horſe-hair, the former to preſerve the moiſture, and the latter as the only ſafeguard againſt the amazing large rats that are in ſuch great abundance in almoſt all ſhips.

It much pleaſed me to obſerve the manner in which the inhabitants kept Holy Thurſday, which they term *La Fête Dieu.* On the evening preceding that day, I could not conceive the reaſon that the people were bringing cart loads of ſmall firs into the city; but judge how great was my ſurprize in the morning, when I went to the parade, to find the ſtreets ſwept as clean as poſſible, theſe trees ſtuck in the ground on each ſide, and ſo contrived that their tops united, that every ſtreet had the appearance of a grove, and upon enquiry found

it

was intended for the celebration of this great feſtival.

About eleven o'clock the proceſſion began from the great Church, which extended near half a mile in length. All the principal Clergy, the Friars of the different Convents, with a large band of muſic attending; in the center of the proceſſion, under a canopy of crimſon velvet, ſupported by ſix Prieſts, the High Prieſt carried the HOST, upon a Bible, covered with a white napkin, and before him two men bore a large baſket full of flowers, which were ſtrewed by ſeveral little boys in ſurplices; four others, with ſilver chalices, were continually wafting the incenſe towards the Hoſt, the people at the ſame time ſinging anthems. In this manner the proceſſion went through moſt of the ſtreets in the city, and thoſe who met it fell inſtantly on their knees; thoſe who remained in their houſes, came to the windows

and

and did the fame. I cannot but fay it was
a pleafing fight, and could not help thinking but it muft be magnificent indeed, in
thofe countries where the Roman Catholic
is the eftablifhed religion.

We were apprized of fome proceffion,
from an order given the day preceding by
General Phillips, but had no idea of feeing
fuch a fpectacle. There having been feveral difputes in Roman Catholic countries,
concerning the refpect that the military
fhould pay the Hoft, when paffing by, his
Majefty, a few years ago, iffued out a general order for that purpofe, which General
Phillips gave out in orders as follows :---
" As to-morrow there will be a great pro-
" ceffion through the city, I need not in-
" form the officers of the refpect and
" attention his Majefty has required fhould
" be paid the Hoft, when paffing. The
" non-commiffioned officers are defired to
" be particular in informing the men, that

VOL. I. P " when

" when the Hoft is going by, they are to
" front it, and behave in a decent and re-
" fpectful manner, to pull off their hats,
" and remain in that fituation till the pro-
" ceffion has paffed.   Any complaint that
" is made to the General, will be punifhed
" with the utmoft feverity."

leaves for La Cole

To-morrow I leave this city, to join the
advanced corps at the river *La Cole*.   Situated as I muft be, confined to the company, which I am proud in faying is commanded by Lord Peterfham, you cannot
expect the whole detail of the manœuvres
of the different actions that may happen,
or a particular account of the fiege of Ticonderoga.   I fhall however inform you
of every thing that comes under my own
obfervation, and give you my opinion of
events, not as an officer, but merely as a
fpectator.

The

The officers take the field under great disadvantages, in regard to horses to transport their baggage, when they quit the Lakes; those for the use of Government are sent through the woods to Crown Point, but their arrival at that place is very uncertain, as they are liable to be taken by the enemy.   It is quite a hazard, but rather than be distressed when I get to Ticonderoga, I have risqued sending mine, with some others, through the woods; if they arrive safe it will be a vast convenience; if not, I shall be compelled to send back my baggage, and then, hey for courage and a knapsack!

Should any misfortune attend the cattle intended for Government, it will greatly retard the army, provided the Americans should abandon Ticonderoga; at all events it will impede us in some measure, as it will be several days after the army gets there before the horses arrive, and you

P 2   may

may eafily conceive an army cannot move without its artillery and provifions.

Another great difadvantage which we experience in the profecution of this war, and which the Americans avoid is, that we have to tranfport all our provifions with us, whereas they have magazines ftored with great abundance, every thirty or forty miles; where, in cafe any difafter attends their army, the lofs of their provifions is eafily recruited. But if any fuch event fhould happen with us, we fhould be obliged to make a ftand at fome ftrong poft, till provifions could be fent from Canada.

Added to this, the Americans are by much our fuperiors at wood-fighting, being habituated to the woods from their infancy. Our fuccefs in any engagement muft greatly reft on the bayonet, the great utility of which General Burgoyne pointed out in an order a few days fince, ftrongly recom-

recommending the officers to inculcate that idea into the minds of the men.

After I leave this city, you muſt not expect to hear from me ſo regularly as you have lately. But you may reſt aſſured, I ſhall embrace every opportunity of letting you know I am not yet food for the crows.

Yours, &c.

P 3 LET-

L E T T E R   XIX.

Montreal, May 26th, 1777.

MY DEAR FRIEND,

A FEW days fince I was invited to
dine with Capt. Frazer, who is fuperintendant over the Indians, and who
gave us a dinner entirely of wild-meats.
Moft of the difhes were only to fet off the
table, there being fuch things there as very
few of the company could partake of; we
had the leg of a bear, indeed, which was
falted, and far exceeded in flavor a leg of
pork; another difh, which though deemed
a great rarity with you, is not efteemed
fuch here, a very fine haunch of venifon.

To

To tell you the truth, I really made my repaſt of what *Monſieur Roberdeau*, of Quebec, hinted to me, of the *Friandiſes*.

Juſt as the cloth was removed, there came into the room a great number of Indians, (and amongſt them one very old) who not having much ceremony, and ſeeing the bottles and glaſſes on the table, would drink with us, and began to be extremely troubleſome, when Capt. Frazer interfered, and to ſhew you the controul he has over them, the inſtant he ſpoke, they quitted the room, but not without a preſent, for I did not underſtand the Indian language, but as I thought, and as he afterwards told us he was obliged to order his ſervant to give them a bottle of rum,

After we had got rid of theſe troubleſome gueſts, and the table reſtored to order, Capt. Frazer ſaid, Gentlemen, I obſerved you all took notice of that old Indian,

P 4   which

which the company acquiefcing in, he
told the following very fingular hiftory relative to him :

That Indian, faid he, is of the *Algouquin*
nation, who are converted to Chriftianity,
and who, being attached to the French, had
excited the enmity of the *Iroquois*, whofe
hatred to Chriftians carried them to every
excefs of fury, murdering and tormenting
to death, without any regard to fex or age,
every one that had the misfortune to fall
into their hands.   To efcape the fury of
the *Iroquois*, the whole nation of the *Algou-*
quins were determined to fight their way to
the French, in which ftruggle the women took no inconfiderable fhare, but
nobly refifted their enemies on this occafion, when it fo happened, that the mother
of that old Indian was taken prifoner.

The *Iroquois* carried her to one of their
villages, ftripped her naked, bound her
hand

hand and foot in one of their cabins, and in that ftate fhe remained for ten days, the favages fleeping round every night. The 11th night, when they were all afleep, fhe difengaged herfelf from the ropes they had bound her with and fled into the foreft. The fecond day after her efcape, her footfteps were perceived by the *Iroquois* who were in fearch of her, and they purfued her with fuch expedition, that the third day fhe difcovered them clofe at her heels : fhe inftantly plunged into a pond of water that was near her, and diving amongft fome weeds and bulrufhes, juft kept her head above water, fo as to breathe, and by this ftratagem efcaped from her purfuers, who, after making a moft diligent fearch, went away the courfe they thought fhe would take. When night came on, fhe left her fituation, and took a different route to that fhe perceived the favages had taken, by which means this poor creature wandered through the woods for five and

thirty

thirty days, without any other fuftenance
than roots and wild-berries. At length
fhe came to the river St. Laurence, and
not perceiving any canoe along the fhore,
made a kind of wicker raft, on which
fhe croffed the river, and had paffed by
Montreal, not knowing well in what part
of the river fhe was, when, perceiving a
canoe full of favages, and fearful left they
might be *Iroquois*, fhe again ran into the
woods, and remained till fun-fet, when
fhe directed her courfe to Montreal.---
Within a mile of the city, fhe was difcovered by a party whom fhe knew to be
Algonquins; when they approached her, fhe
fquatted down behind a bufh, calling out
to them that fhe was not in a condition to
be feen, as fhe was naked; one of them
then threw her a blanket, and conducted
her into the fort. After Capt. Frazer had
related this ftory, he told us this old Indian took great pleafure in telling it to
every one, at the fame time expreffing the
utmoft

utmoſt indignation, and vowing revenge againſt the *Iroquois*.

We had ſcarcely drank five glaſſes, after Captain Frazer had finiſhed his narration, when the Indians returned, upon a pretence of buſineſs to him, which was no other than that of procuring more rum, which Captain Frazer refuſing them, they grew extremely troubleſome, and what, with the liquor they had already drank, were much beyond any controul, for they paid no attention to Capt. Frazer, who, finding he could not pacify, or any way get rid of them, made us an apology, and the company broke up.

On my return home, mentioning to my landlord what I had heard concerning the *Iroquois*, he ſaid, *Monſieur, les Iroquois ſont le plus ſauvage et frauduleux de tout*, and related the ſad cataſtrophe of a Miſſionary, one *Father Jogues*, who reſided a little below

low *Trois Rivieres* : imagining he had made great progrefs in converting them to Chriftianity, during a fhort interval of peace, was willing to fpread his doctrine amongft the remote of the *Iroquois*; for that purpofe, he fet out with four Indians, and a young Frenchman as his fervant; he had not paffed *Trois Rivieres* above a league, when his four favage guides abandoned them: yet fuch was his enthufiafm and confidence of having wrought upon them fo far, that his perfon was in fafety, he would not return, but travelled on, and at the very firft *Iroquois* village he and his fervant came to, he was too fatally convinced of his error, for they were feized, ftript, fcourged, buffeted, and treated as prifoners of war. At this fudden change the good Father was in great amazement, and began (for he could fpeak their language) to expoftulate with all the powers of elocution, which were of no avail, and the only favor that his eloquence could

procure

procure him was, that inftead of burning him and his companion alive, they humanely condefcended to behead them with a hatchet. After my landlord had finifhed the ftory, he faid, with great warmth and indignation, *Monfieur, les Iroquois font frauduleux comme le Diable, et en voyagent j'ai toujours crainte de le rencontre*; and, from the ftory he had related, you will no doubt fay he had very good foundation for his fears.

I am, yours, &c.

LET-

L E T T E R XX.

Montreal, May 31*ſt*, 1777.

MY DEAR FRIEND,

BEFORE I leave this city, though there is not much leiſure time on my hands, I ſhall communicate to you the fruit of my enquiries (to which I have applied myſelf this winter) reſpecting the advantage England derives from Canada.

It was a complaint, and perhaps not without foundation, that Canada never enriched France, and that none of its inhabitants acquired the leaſt fortunes, but the Indian traders. As it was not the

fault

fault of the country, which has many ftaple commodities, from which a fource of wealth might be derived, whence then is to be attributed this caufe? Firft, from the continual ftate of warfare this province has been in from its very firft fettlement; to the oppreffivenefs of the government, and the rapacioufnefs of the clergy; from which caufes (except thofe enterprizing people who embark in the fur trade) the inhabitants not having a ftimulative motive, were content with a mere exiftence, and if a Canadian could but pay his tythes and duties to his prieft, and lay up a little to enjoy a long tedious winter, his happinefs was compleat.

But the fcene is now reverfed; all over the province there are faw and grift-mills, and the Canadians are now enriching themfelves, by exporting lumber and grain to the Weft Indies and the other provinces. As I obferved before, it was not the fault

of

of the country, for to perfons induftrioufly inclined, this country has many advantages, as after they have tilled their ground in autumn, from that time till the middle of April and the begining of May, when they fow their crops, they have to cut down timber, and to faw it for building, fhipping, and other ufes, ready for exportation when the froft breaks up. Another great advantage this country poffeffes, is the quick vegetation, for the crop that is fown in May fprings up, grows to perfection, is cut down and carried into the barns by the end of Auguft.

Without confidering the hardfhips and difficulties they were expofed to, the Indian trader was always looked upon with an envious eye: but now, as they are not liable to the rapacity of ftate and clergy, but enjoy all the privileges of our happy conftitution, their induftry is very great, and thofe winters that ufed to be fpent in
feafting

feafting and pleafure, is now employed to more ufeful purpofes, and an Indian trader is not now a man fo much to be envied.

Daily experience fhews, that this province is capable of producing more refources than one. What motives of policy could it be in the French to keep the Canadians in fuch a ftate of oppreffion? It fhould feem that France was fufficiently proud in having this vaft territory annexed to its crown, and content with the produce of the fur trade. But left you think I am entering too deeply into politics, I fhall conclude, deferring to my next an account of the fur trade, which ftill is the greateft refource of wealth to England, but which muft in procefs of time be annihilated, from the very great deftruction of the animals, which every year diminifhes them fo faft, and occafions their flying to remoter parts, that the trader has hundreds of leagues farther to go in fearch of them; the neceffity, therefore of encouraging hufbandry, will appear evident to you. But I fee I am again running into politics, therefore adieu.

Yours, &c.

L E T T E R   XXI.

Montreal, June 3d, 1777.

MY DEAR FRIEND,

I NOW proceed to give you fome account of the fur trade, and as in one of my former letters the nature of Indian traders were defcribed to you and their modes of trafficking with the favages, I fhall give you fome little account of the beafts, whofe furs they go in fearch of, and hope you will not think any little remarks that I may interfperfe, as dictating to your fuperior fenfe and underftanding, but merely ideas that occur to me whilft writing.

Q 2   By

By the accounts moſt authors have given
us of Canada, they deſcribe it, upon its firſt
diſcovery, to have been an immenſe tract
of foreſt, ſerving only as an extenſive haunt
to wild beaſts, with which it was over-run,
and which had multiplied prodigiouſly;
for thoſe few men who did inhabit thoſe
deſerts, not having any flocks or tame animals, left more room and food for thoſe
that were wandering and free, like themſelves; and although there was no great
variety, ſtill there were multitudes of each
ſpecies. But they, as every thing, ſooner or
later, in this terreſtrial globe, paid tribute
to the ſovereignty of man; that cruel
power that has been ſo fatal to every living
creature, and the few that the natives deſtroyed for their food and cloathing, were
of little note in ſuch a prodigious multi-
tude. No ſooner had our luxury led us
to make uſe of their ſkins, than the natives
waged a perpetual war againſt them, which
they carried on with great eagerneſs, as in
return

return for the havoc and deftruction they made amongft them, they indulged in a plenty and variety of gratifications they were before unaccuftomed to; and to render the war the more deftructive, we affifted them with fire-arms, by the means of which great quantities of furs, and of a prodigious variety, were procured. Moft of thefe were known in Europe, which were the fame as thofe that came from the northern parts of our hemifphere, but they were in too fmall quantities to fupply a great demand.

Caprice and novelty has made thefe furs more or lefs in fafhion, and England has found it to be for the intereft of Canada, that they fhould be valued at home; and that they are fo with a witnefs, the enormous price your fifter gave for a muff and tippet, is a convincing proof: here I affure you they are very dear, the commoneft fur cap ftanding you in two guineas.

Q 3   As

Having given you a little hiftory of furs, I fhall now defcribe to you fome of the beafts whofe fkins are ftill in requeft, and firft begin with the Otter, which is fo generally known in England, as to need no defcription; there is no other difference than that it is much larger, and its hair blacker and finer than ours, a circumftance fatal to them, as expofing them more to the purfuit of the favages.

The Pole-cat, of which there are three fpecies, is in great eftimation among the Canadian hunters, as the hair is darker, more gloffy, and more filky than thofe in Europe.

Even the Rat of North-America is valuable for its fkin; but the two principal ones that are in the article of trade is the Oppoffum and the Mufk; many and ridiculous are the ftories which are propagated relative to the female of the former, fuch as,

among othrs, that of the young ones getting into the belly again through the teats,
the fact is this, under its belly there
is a loose skin, with a small aperture in
the center, and this she can expand or
deprefs at will; if purfued, and she thinks
her young are in danger, she puts them
into this bag, and runs away with them up
a tree. Another fingular inftance of fagacity in this animal, which is feldom mentioned, is, that if purfued by other animals,
fuch as the Tiger, Mountain-cat, &c. that
can mount trees, it goes to the extremity
of a bough, and fufpends itfelf by its tail.
The fkin of the Mufk-rat is employed for
the fame purpofes as the Beaver, of which
he feems to be a diminutive ; but its moft
intrinfic value is for that predominant and
powerful perfume it produces, and which
is called after this animal.

The Ermine is about the fize of a fquirrel,
but not fo long, has the fame lively eyes,

keen

look, and his motions are fo quick, that
the eye can fcarcely follow them, it has a
long bufhy tail, which at the tip is as black
as jet; what enables me to give you fo
exact a defcription of this little animal is,
that the daughter of the gentleman at
whofe houfe I lodge, has one in her poffeffion; indeed it is the fafhion for the young
ladies to keep them, as ours do fquirrels.
One thing not a little extraordinary of this
animal is, that all the winter it was white
as fnow, and the other day, when admir-
ing it, I expreffed a furprize in perceiving
it had a yellow tint, when the young lady
faid, *Ah! Monfieur, au milieu de l'été c'eft
jaune comme d'or*. This little animal is
reckoned one of the beauties of Canada,
for though the fable is fmaller, it is not fo
common.

The Martin, whofe fkin is the moft valuable, is only to be met with in the center
of the forefts, far from any habitation,
and

and although fo fmall an animal, is a beaft
of prey, living entirely upon birds.   It is
but a foot and a half long, yet leaves a
print in the fnow, which appears to be
the footftep of a larger animal, occafioned
by its jumping along and giving the marks
of both feet together: their fur is much
efteemed, but is inferior to that fpecies
which are called fables, whofe fkins are
of a fhining black.   Thofe of the Martin
encreafe in value from the various dyes,
the deeper the tint the more valuable, and
they gradually encreafe from a light brown
to the deep gloffy black of the fable.   The
Martins feldom more than once in two or
three years quit their receffes in thefe im-
penetrable woods, and when they do, the
Canadians take it as a fign of a good winter, imagining there will be great quantities of fnow, and confequently good fport
in deftroying them.

The

The Wild-cat of Canada is reckoned much fmaller than thofe upon the northern continent of Europe, and is the fame kind of animal that was called by the ancients the Lynx, of which an erroneous opinion has ever prevailed amongft the vulgar, that it is poffeffed of the power of piercing to death with its eyes whatever it deftines for its prey, as nature had deprived it of the faculties of hearing and fmelling at a diftance, which miftaken notion muft have arifen from this fimple caufe, that as this animal lives upon what game it can catch, it will purfue it to the very tops of the talleft trees, and nature having endowed it with a quicker fight than moft other animals, whatever it purfues, though of ever fo fmall a nature, it never lofes fight of, let the foliage of the trees be ever fo thick. The flefh of this animal is very white, and faid to be well flavored, but the Indians hunt it chiefly for its fkin, the hair of it being long, and of a fine light grey,

grey, but not fo valuable as that of the fox.

This animal, like other natives of the frozen climates, where nature produces but few vegetables, is carniverous.

Befides the fmall furs, Canada fupplies England with the fkins of the Stag, Deer, Roebuck, the Caribou and the Elk, the latter of which is fuppofed to be the original of all thefe fpecies. All thefe animals are hunted by the Canadians, but the chace of the Bear the favages have referved to themfelves, and which is their favorite fport; it feems beft adapted to their warlike manners, ftrength and bravery, and efpecially as thofe animals fupply moft of their wants.

Fearful left you may grow tired of this heavy detail of wild beafts, I fhall conclude this, referving to my next the defcription

of

of the only two that are worthy of notice, the Bear and the Beaver, the latter of which poffeffes all the friendly difpofitions, divefted of all the vices and misfortunes that await us, and which debars us from the true and real pleafures arifing from the friendly and fweet intercourfe that fhould fubfift between man and man.

Yours, &c.

L E T-

LETTER XXII.

Montreal, June 7th, 1777.

MY DEAR FRIEND,

OPPORTUNITIES almoſt daily occur-ing, I am happy to embrace them, during the little time I have to remain in this city; when I quit it, you will think me very remiſs in addreſſing you. Let me ſincerely aſſure you, although there will be no regular conveyance, I ſhall embrace every opportunity that offers.

As in my laſt I mentioned to you that the ſavages were ſupplied with moſt of their wants from the Bear, feeding upon

its

its flefh, rubbing themfelves with its greafe, and cloathing themfelves with its fkin, it may not be amifs to give you fome little account of this animal, and the fingular method they have of deftroying them.

As no doubt you muft have feen many of them in England, I fhall only give you an account of fome of its particularities.

This animal is rather fhy than fierce, and will feldom attack a man; on the contrary, they will fly at the fight of him, and a dog will drive them a great way. The only time they are dangerous is after having been wounded, when they quit the hollow trees they have refided in all the winter, and at the time of rutting, which is in the month of July; they are then fo fierce and ill-tempered, the effects of jealoufy, that they are extremely dangerous to meet with. At this feafon they grow very lean, and their flefh has fo difagreeable a relifh, that the Indians, whofe

whofe ftomachs are none of the moft delicate, will not touch it. Who could conceive that an animal, fo unlovely in its appearance, fhould in the fpace of one month
grow leaner by the *belle paſſion*, than after
an abftinence of fix months.

But the feafon over, he recovers his former *embonpoint*, which he is greatly affifted
in regaining by the great quantity of fruits
the woods abound with, and of which he
is extremely greedy; grapes he is particularly fond of, climbing after them up the
moft lofty trees. After he has fed for fome
time on fruits, his flefh becomes delicious,
and continues fo till fpring.

It is furprizing enough that this animal,
although provided with fo warm a fur,
and not of the moft delicate appearance,
fhould take more precautions than any
other to preferve itfelf from the cold,
(this may ferve as a leffon from nature,
not

not to form our judgment of things by appearance, fince every one is the beft judge of his own wants;) for which pur-pofe, when the winter fets in, he climbs up the hollow rotten trunk of an old tree, ftopping up the entrance with pine branches, by which means he is fheltered from all inclemencies of the weather, and when once lodged, he feldom or ever quits his apartment during the winter, which is the more fingular, it being certain that he lays up no manner of provifion, and that he muft require fome nourifhment. That he requires little food is natural to fuppofe, as at the end of autumn he is very fat, takes no exercife, and almoft always fleeps, and, therefore, lofing little by perfpiration, has very feldom occafion to go abroad in queft of it, and when he does, haftens back to his retreat. A ridiculous notion is gone abroad into the world, that during the winter the fole nourifhment of the Bear is licking its paws, which, no doubt, arofe from

from the amazing long time thefe animals can, either through the nourifhment they receive from fleep, or idlenefs, go without food. Yet that fuch an idea fhould prevail, I am not furprized, as there has been an inftance of one that was chained for a whole winter without either food or drink, and at the end of fix months was found as fat as when firft caught.

The feafon for hunting the bear is in winter, when the Indians force him from his habitation by fetting fire to the pine branches that he has drawn together at the bottom of the hollow tree, when the fmoke afcending up the trunk, drives him from his late comfortable habitation, from which he no fooner defcends, than they kill him. The Indians now only deftroy them to anfwer their own wants, as formerly they ufed to do for the purpofe of difpofing of their fkins to the traders; but it was no fooner underftood that

Vol. I.   R   Canada

Canada was ftored with Beavers, than the favages, urged on by a more lucrative intereft, directed their war againft an animal the moft harmlefs, who molefts no living creature, and is neither carniverous nor fanguinary. This is, I am forry to obferve, become an object of man's moft earneft purfuit, and the one that the favages hunt after with the greateft eagernefs and cruelty; a circumftance entirely owing to the unmerciful rapacioufnefs which luxury has made neceffary in fkins, for all the polifhed nations of Europe.

This animal is by nature adapted for focial life, being endowed with an inftinct in the prefervation and propagation of its fpecies; it is generally about three or four feet long, moftly weighing from forty to fixty pounds; the hinder feet are webbed, which enables it to fwim, and in the fore feet the toes are divided; its tail is oval, very flat, and covered with fcales; the head refembles

refembles that of a rat, in which are four very fharp teeth, with thefe it will gnaw through trees of a great circumference.

This animal is divefted of turbulent paffions, without a defire of doing injury to any one, free from craft, fcarcely defending itfelf, unlefs it lives in fociety; it never bites, except when caught, and as nature has not fupplied it with any weapons of defence, by a natural inftinct as it were, it forms focieties, and has various contrivances to fecure its eafe, without fighting, and to live without committing, or fuffering an injury; although this peaceable, and you may fay almoft tame animal, enters into fociety, it is neverthelefs independent, every want being fupplied by itfelf, and therefore it is a flave to none. It will not ferve, nor does it pretend to command, every care feems directed by an inftinct, that at the fame time, as it labors for the general good, it lives for itfelf

R 2   alone.

alone. To learn the nature of the focieties of thefe animals, as it was related to me by my landlord, may afford you the fame entertainment it did me.

In the month of June or July, they affemble from all quarters, to the number of two or three hundred, near fome lake or pool of water, to build their habitations againft winter, the conftruction of which, from the complication and manner of difpofing the materials, one would be led to imagine to be beyond the capacity of any one but an intelligent being, and efpecially in their conftructing of dams, when they cannot meet with a lake or pool; in this cafe they fix upon fome river, when the firft of their labour is to make a dam, which they generally do in the fhalloweft part of the ftream, for that purpofe felling trees with the four fharp teeth that I have already defcribed; five or fix of them will gnaw a large
one

one through, and to mark to you the wonderful fagacity of thefe induftrious brutes, they contrive it fo that it always falls in the water: having laid this foundation, they fell fmaller trees, which they roll to this great one, but what appears the moft wonderful is, the manner they fink the piles in the water, to prevent the ftream's carrying away the trees, they lay acrofs. Their contrivance is this, with their nails they dig a hole in the ground, or at the bottom of the water, with their teeth they reft the ftake againft the bank of the river, or againft the tree that lies acrofs, and with their feet they raife the ftake and fink it with the fharp end (which thefe fenfible animals make to it) in the hole that they have made, where it ftands up; and to render thefe ftakes or piles more fecure, they interweave branches of fmall trees, and with their tails wifk up a kind of mortar with clay, and fill the vacant fpace of the interwoven branches.

R 3 After

After this work is finifhed by the body at
large, each one confiders of fome lodging
for himfelf; an hut being built upon piles
on the fides of the Lake, capable of containing from two or three to ten or fifteen,
(for they divide themfelves into companies, and build thefe huts accordingly;)
which are formed with walls and parti-
tions of about two feet thick and as many
in height, arched over, and the whole
fo plaiftered with clay, that the fmalleft
breath of air cannot penetrate through
them; each apartment is made large
enough to contain two, a male and female; each hut has two entrances, one
towards the land, and the other on the
fide towards the ftream, the former for
them to go into the woods to fetch provifions, and the latter to efcape from their
enemy, that is to fay MAN, the deftroyer
of cities and commonwealths. The infide of
their apartments has no other furniture
than the flooring of grafs covered with
                                    the

the boughs of the fir, and thefe animals
are fo cleanly, that no filth of any kind
is ever feen in thefe apartments.

In each hut there are ftore houfes pro-
portionate to the number of its inhabitants;
every one knows its own, and never fteals
from his neighbour. Each party, that is to
fay, the male and female, live in their own
habitations; they have no jealoufies or
quarrels; the provifions of the community
are collected and expended without any
conteft, and reft fatisfied with the fimple
food that their labors procure them.   The
only paffion they have is that of conjugal
affection, wherein a moft excellent example is held forth to that all-wife and all-
fufficient man, who is led away by every
guft of paffion and vanity.

Two of thefe animals, in the courfe of
their labours in the fummer months, match
together, unite by inclination and re-

R 4   ciprocal

ciprocal choice, and agree to pafs the winter, and like too many couple who haftily enter into matrimony with equally as good motives, but forgetting what fhould make the happinefs lafting, that of laying up a ftock to guard againft an inclement feafon.

The happy couple retire to their hut about the end of autumn, which has been obferved to be no lefs favorable to love than fpring; for if the feafon of flowers invites the feathered tribe to propagate in the woods, the feafon of fruits as powerfully excites the inhabitants of the earth in the reproduction of their fpecies; befides, as winter gives leifure for amorous purfuits, it compenfates for the advantages of other feafons.

I am this moment told that the pacquet is going to fail, and muft therefore defer a further account of this wonderful and surprizing furprizing animal, from whom fo many leffons of induftry and morality may be drawn, till another opportunity, and conclude with affuring you of my beft wifhes for your happinefs and profperity, and that I remain

Yours, &c.

LET-

LETTER   XXIII.

Montreal, *June* 8th, 1777.

MY DEAR FRIEND,

I SEND this by our friend Captain F. who is going poſt to Quebec, from which place he will ſail immediately, and as the navigation from this city to Quebec is much delayed by the various currents and other cauſes in the river, he will be there as ſoon, if not ſooner, than the ſhip I ſent my firſt by, in which caſe you may receive this before the other, which may greatly bewilder you. I therefore ſhall juſt hint to you, this is the concluſion of the hiſtory of the Beaver.

If

If my recollection does not deceive me,
I left off in my laſt at deſcribing his love,
that univerſal paſſion of nature, which the
Beaver ſeems to enjoy in the conjugal ſtate,
comparatively much happier than mankind; for when they couple and enter their
huts, they never quit each other, confe-
crating their whole time to love, from
which neither labor nor any other object
can divert them.

If by chance a ſun-ſhiny day ſhould
happen to enliven the gloomy melancholy
of the ſeaſon, the happy couple leave their
huts to walk on the borders of the Lake,
regaling themſelves with ſome freſh bark,
and breathing the ſalutary exhalations of
the earth.   At the concluſion of the winter, the mother brings forth the endearing
pledges of their affection, while the father
ranges the woods, allured by the ſweets of
the ſpring, leaving to his little family
that portion of room which he took up in
his

his narrow cell. The Beaver generally
produces two or three, which the mother
fuckles, nurfes and trains up, for when the
father is abfent, fhe takes out the young
ones, in her excurfions for cray and other
fifh, and green bark to recruit her own
ftrength and to feed her young, till the
feafon of labor returns ; for although thefe
animals are fo induftrious as to build themfelves habitations that would laft them a
century, they are obliged to rebuild them
every year, as the firft thing the traders do
when they meet with any of their works,
is to break down their cabins and the dam,
together with their dyke.

There are various methods of taking and
deftroying thefe animals, by draining the
water from their dykes, and fometimes by
fnares ; they are very feldom fhot at, for
unlefs killed on the fpot, they are loft to
the huntfman, by plunging into the water
wounded, when they fink to the bottom
                                        and

and never rife. The moft certain and general mode of catching them is by fetting
traps in the woods, where they perceive
them to have been eating the bark of the
young trees; they bait thefe traps with
frefh flips of wood, which the Beaver no
fooner touches, than a great weight falls
and crufhes its loins, when the huntfman,
who lies concealed near the fpot, haftens
to kill it.

No doubt but by this time you are
heartily tired with fo long a detail of this
animal; but if I have deviated from the
common path of defcription, I can only
fay it has proceeded from thefe two caufes,
that I cannot fufficiently admire the many
virtues it poffeffes, divefted of all manner
of vice, and have been loft in the contem-
plation of that Divine Being, who formed
it with all thefe natural endowments.

You

You muſt pardon my making a compa-
riſon between the ſocieties of theſe animals
and thoſe of a convent.   If happineſs may
be ſaid to dwell in both communities, it
muſt be allowed to be by very oppoſite
means.   The happineſs of one conſiſts in
following the dictates of nature; in the
other, nature, the ſweets of ſocial love, and
the laws of our creation, are totally deſtroyed!   The inſtitution of the ſociety of
the Beaver, ſeems ſolely to propagate its
ſpecies; the other to annihilate it.   How
many, who might have dignified nature
under the character of a fond mother and
an affectionate wife, are loſt to the world
and to themſelves!---they cannot help feeling tender emotions, and, in the bitterneſs
of miſery, execrate that tyrant cuſtom,
which has torn them from the embraces of
happineſs and chained them in cells, a prey
to affections hopeleſs and inſatiable---the
idea carries me beyond myſelf.

What

What will not the feelings of humanity exclaim, when it confiders that thefe gloomy and ferocious inftitutions are wafting away in all parts of Europe! Inftitutions not only injurious but inhuman, which, under the abfurd and ridiculous notion of making men equal to angels, robs health of its vigor, and beauty of its reward.

I am moft agreeably interrupted in my ferious reflections, by a vifit from our friend S----, who is juft arrived from New-York; he was taken prifoner in the courfe of laft fummer, by a notorious fellow of the name of Whitcomb, the fame man who fhot Brigadier General Gordon, the particulars of which I fhall inform you in my next.

Yours, &c.

LET-

LETTER   XXIV.

Montreal, June 12th, 1777.

MY DEAR FRIEND,

IN my laft I mentioned to you the name
of one Whitcomb, a native of Connecticut, and a great partizan of the Americans, who, after the defeat upon the Lakes,
offered his fervice to venture through the
woods, and bring in prifoner an Englifh
officer, for which purpofe he ftationed himfelf among the thickeft copfes that are between *La Prairé* and St. John's.   The firft
officer who happened to pafs him was
Brigadier General Gordon ; he was mounted on a fpirited horfe, and Whitcomb
thinking

thinking there was little probability of feizing him, fired at and wounded him in the fhoulder. The General immediately rode as faft as he could to the camp at St. John's, which he had but juft reached, when with lofs of blood and fatigue, he fell from his horfe; fome foldiers, took him up and carried him to the hofpital, where, after his wound was dreffed, and he was a little at eafe, he related the circumftance, which being immediately made known to General Carleton, a party of Indians were fent out to fcour the woods, and fearch for Whitcomb, but in vain, as he haftened back to Ticonderoga. General Carleton, however, imagining he might be lurking about the woods, or fecreted in the houfe of fome difaffected Canadian, iffued out a proclamation among the inhabitants, offering a reward of fifty guineas to any one that would bring Whitcomb, alive or dead, to the camp.

A few days after this General Gordon died of his wound, in whofe death we fincerely lamented the lofs of a brave and experienced officer.

When Whitcomb returned to Ticonderoga, and informed the General who commanded there, that although he could not take an officer prifoner, he believed he had mortally wounded one, the General expreffed his difapprobation in the higheft terms, and was fo much difpleafed at the tranfaction, that Whitcomb, in order to effect a reconciliation, offered his fervice to go again, profeffing he would forfeit his life, if he did not return with a prifoner.

He accordingly, with two other men, proceeded down Lake *Champlain*, in a canoe, to a fmall creek, where they fecreted it, and repaired to the woods, to the fame fpot where Whitcomb had ftationed himfelf before ; the two men lay concealed a little

way

way in the wood, whilft he fkulked about the borders of it.

The regiment of which our friend S---- is Quarter-mafter, having occafion for fome ftores from Montreal, he was going from the campt at St. John's to procure them; he was advifed not to go this road, but by way of *Chamblée*, on account of the late accident, but you know him to be a man of great bravery and perfonal courage, joined with uncommon ftrength; refolving not to go fo many miles out of his road for any Whitcomb whatever, he jocofely added, that he fhould be very glad to meet with him, as he was fure he fhould get the reward; in this, however, he was greatly miftaken, his reward being noother than that of being taken prifoner himfelf.

Previous to his fetting out he took every precaution, having not only loaded his fufée, but charged a brace of piftols; when

S 2   he

he came near to the woods I have already
ſcribed, he was very cautious, but in an
inſtant, Whitcomb and the two men he
had with him ſprung from behind a thick
buſh, and ſeized him before he could make
the leaſt reſiſtance ; they then took from
him his fuſée and piſtols, tied his arms behind him with ropes, and blind-folded him.

It was three days before they reached the
canoe that had been concealed, during which
time they had but very ſcanty fare ; a few
hard biſcuits ſerved to allay hunger, while
the fruit of the woods was a luxury !---
When Whitcomb had marched him to ſuch
a diſtance as he thought he could not make
his eſcape, were he at liberty, through fear
of loſing himſelf, for the greater eaſe on
his own part, and to facilitate their march,
they untied his hands, and took the cloth
from his eyes. Only picture to yourſelf
what muſt have been his feelings, at ſeeing
himſelf in the midſt of a thick wood, ſur-
rounded

rounded by three defperate fellows, and uncertain as to their intentions!

At night, when they had partaken of their fcanty pittance, two out of the three ufed to fleep, whilft the other kept watch. The firft night he flept through fatigue; on the fecond, as you may naturally fup-pofe, from his great anxiety of mind, he could not clofe his eyes, in the middle of which an opportunity occurred whereby he could have effected his efcape, for the man whofe watch it was, fell faft afleep. He has fince told me how his mind waver-ed for a length of time, what meafures to purfue; he could not bear the idea of put-ting them to death, though juftified by the rules of war: if he efcaped from them, they might in all probability retake and ill-treat him. The great hazard of all, which determined him to abide by his fate was, that by being fo many miles in a tract of wood, where he could not tell what

S 3   direction

direction to take (having been blind-folded
when he entered it) he might poffibly wan-
der up and down till he perifhed with hunger. In this reftlefs ftate, he remained
till day-break, when they refumed their
march, and in the evening came to the
creek where the canoe was concealed; they
then fecured him again, put him in the
canoe, and proceeded up the lake to Ticonderoga, where they arrived early the
next morning. When they landed him
he was again blind-folded, that he might
not fee their works, and thus conducted to
the General, whofe only motive for endeavouring to get an officer was, either by
threats or intreaties, to gain information
relative to our army. In this, however, he
was greatly difappointed, and as he could
not obtain the leaft intelligence from our
friend, he ordered him as prifoner of war
upon his parole, to fome of the interior
towns, from which place, as I informed
you in my laft, he is juft returned, as
                                        hearty

hearty and well as ever. I fhould not have dwelt fo long on this fubject, but knowing you have his welfare fo much at heart, that you feel yourfelf interefted in whatever concerns him.

I fhall now conclude, but before I do fo, let me congratulate you on the recovery of your health, after fo alarming an illnefs. Good health alone fweetens life, and that you may long enjoy it, both for your own fake and that of your friends, is the ardent wifh of

Yours, &c.

LET-

L E T T E R　XXV.

Camp at St. John's, June 14th, 1777.

MY DEAR FRIEND,

I HAD scarcely finished my last, when I received orders to march to this place, and am now entering upon the hurry and bustle of an active campaign. You must not accuse me now of inattention, if you should not hear from me so frequently.

As I observed in a former letter, it was the general opinion the King's troops would not be prevented passing Lake *Champlain*, but wait our arrival at Ticonderoga; in that case the operations of the campaign

will

will commence at Crown Point. It would be doing great injuſtice to thoſe who have been ſtationed at this garriſon during the winter, if I omitted to mention their great exertions in repairing, augmenting, and rendering fit for immediate ſervice the *batteaux*, gun-boats, and armed veſſels. The other parts of the army have been equally as induſtrious in eſtabliſhing magazines at Montreal, Sorell and *Chamblée*, which muſt be effeɕted during the froſt, not only as the conveyance is eaſier at that time, but on account of the roads, which, by the running and melting of the ſnow, are generally impaſſable for ſome months.

By all the accounts that can be colleɕted, the Americans are in great force at Ticonderoga, nearly to the amount of 12,000, and a conſiderable number occupy Lake George, ſuſtained by a great naval power, with a view, no doubt, of ſecuring their retreat

in cafe they fhould be obliged to abandon
Ticonderoga.

Should the navigation of Lake *Champlain*
be fecured by the fuperiority of our naval
force, the advanced corps, under the command of General Frafer, with a large body
of favages and Canadians, for fcouts and
out-works, and the beft of our engineers
and artificers, are to take poffeffion of
Crown Point, and to fortify it. The intention is with a view to prevent infult
from the enemy, during the time neceffary
for collecting ftores, forming magazines
and fortifying pofts, all which muft be accomplifhed previous to our proceeding in
force to lay fiege to Ticonderoga.

This brigade being ftationed at Crown
Point, as a check on the enemy, the reft of
the army are to be employed in forwarding
the convoys and tranfports of provifions,
removing artillery, preparing fafcines and
other

other neceffaries for artillery operations, and to commence the fiege; and that the enemy during that period may not reft in tranquillity, corps of favages, fupported by detachments of the light infantry, are to keep them in continual alarm within their works, at the fame time to cover reconnoitering parties, both of general officers and engineers, and to obtain the beft intelligence of their ftrength, pofition and defign. From the great preparations that have been made during the winter, and by the vigorous exertion of the troops, who are in great health and fpirits, it may reafonably be expected that the reduction of Ticonderoga will be early in the fummer, unlefs fome misfortune, human prudence cannot forefee, fhould prevent it, although it is the general opinion it will be warmly contefted, and that there will be much blood-fhed. The Americans, when they drew the fword, muft have forefeen a bloody conteft, and expected all the horrors of a

war,

war, carried on as it were in their own
bofoms, laying wafte their fields of harveft, deftroying every comfort, and intro-
ducing every mifery mankind is capable of
devifing. But had certain perfons, who
were actuated by no other motives than a
welfare and profperity to both countries,
directed their refolves, they would have
advifed a peaceable fubmiffion to the Mother Country, and eafily prevented all the
horrors of a civil war. America, from
a number of aggregate fortunate circumftances, by flow degrees, had arifen to a
ftate of great profperity, and the power
that fhe had fixed by that profperity, bids
fair to be of fome duration, yet, in my
opinion, not to fuch a degree as to eftablifh
her independence; her prefent diftreffed
fituation, without fome other favorable
circumftance, muft inevitably prevent the
execution of that idea. I am fully perfuaded in my own mind, had they but
referved their ideas of independency for
half

half a century longer, from their increafe of population and wealth, they would have fixed it without much difficulty, or even the affiftance of any other power, and thus become the firft nation in the world.   In the prefent day, if they attain their boafted end, it muft be by the arm of fome nation, to whom, for want of refources to defray the expences of their alliance, fhe will be in continual broils and difputes, which may perhaps finally terminate in a total fubjection, and that abject flavery they fo ridiculoufly pretend to dread from us. Should this be the cafe, fhe will regret the lofs of that protection from the Mother Country, fhe is now treating with fo much ingratitude. Leaving you to your own re-marks, for no doubt you will fay, "a foldier and a politician!" I fhall divert your atten-tion from the cabals of mankind, to the wonderful productions of nature, in de-fcribing to you a little animal that was brought me lately, called a flying-fquirrel.

This

This animal takes its name from being provided with a fkin, or membrane, which adheres to each fide, about the breadth of three inches, extending from its hind to fore feet, where it is connected by a bony articulation ; it expands this membrane like a fail, by which it is enabled to fly from one tree to another, at a great diftance. Moft fquirrels will jump from tree to tree, when contiguous, but this animal will fly an incredible way. Its fkin is very foft, and of a beautiful dark grey, with eyes large, black, and very prominent; it fomewhat differs from the other fquirrels in its tafte, caring little for nuts, the chief and favorite food being the frefh tops of the birch. This little animal makes its bed in a very curious manner, of the mofs of the fame tree, in which it lies as it were buried, feldom ftirring from thence in the day time, unlefs difturbed. I came into poffeffion of it from a little drum-boy's going up a tree after a bird's neft, who

perceiving

perceiving it lay in that dormitory ſtate, ſeized it and brought it to me, for he had heard that I was making a collection of natural curioſities. By the bye, I beg you will inform me, in your next, if you received ſafe the little collection I ſent you from Montreal. I have added this curious animal, and one of another ſpecies, called the ground ſquirrel, which is a little larger than a mouſe, and moſt beautifully ſpotted like a fawn, to the collection I am now making, and hope they will be conſidered as tokens of friendſhip from

Yours, &c.

LET-

L E T T E R   XXVI.

Camp at River Bouquet, } *June* 23, 1777,
upon Lake Champlain,

MY DEAR FRIEND,

WE have proceeded thus far, and, from all appearance, shall traverse the remainder of our way on the Lake, without meeting any oppofition from the enemy, their defign being, as I before mentioned to you, to difpute Ticonderoga; the intelligence from different fpies and deferters fully confirm us in this opinion, who report, that they have labored hard to ftrengthen, and mean to difpute it moft vigoroufly. They are now building row-gallies at Fort George, for the defence

defence of that lake, and fortifying the road to Skenefborough.

It feems the Congrefs have configned to the four New England provinces, as they are excellent axe-men, and very expeditious in felling of trees, the tafk of fupplying men and provifion to oppofe the progrefs of our forces, which they have undertaken, upon condition of being exempt from fupplying General Wafhington's army. If that really is the cafe, we fhall have bufinefs enough upon our hands, having four of the moft powerful and rebellious provinces to deal with; they have this advantage too, that upon their frontiers, fhould any difafter befall them, it can be fo eafily recruited, both as to men and provifions.

Having proceeded thus far up the lake, I am enabled to give you fome account of it, efpecially as we have paffed the broadeft part. There are many fmall iflands dif-

Vol. I.   T   perfed

perfed in different parts, and where it is
wideft, you are not able to difcern the
oppofite fhore; there are feveral plantations on each fide, but they are more
numerous on the fouth, the north fide
being lofty rocky mountains. It abounds
with great quantities and variety of fifh;
fturgeon, black bafs, mafquenongez, pike
of an incredible fize, and many others,
among which is a cat-fifh, which is about
eighteen inches long, of a brownifh caft,
without fcales, having a large round head,
refembling that of a cat's, from which it
derives its name; they have on their heads
protuberances fimilar to the horns of a
fnail, and like them can elevate and deprefs them at pleafure, and when fully
extended, are about two inches long; if in
liberating one of thefe fifh from the hook,
it ftrikes you with one of its horns, it
leaves an unaccountable and unpleafant
fenfation on the part affected for two or
three days. Its fins are very bony and
ftrong,

ftrong, like thofe of a perch, it commonly weighs about five or fix pounds; the flefh is fat and lufcious, greatly refembling the flavor of an eel.

There are at this feafon of the year prodigious flights of pigeons croffing the lake, of a moft beautiful plumage, and in aftonifhing quantities.

Thefe are moft excellent eating, and that you may form fome idea as to their number, at one of our encampments, the men for one day wholly fubfifted on them; fatigued with their flight in croffing the lake, they alight upon the firft branch they can reach to, many are fo weary as to drop in the water, and are eafily caught; thofe that alight upon a bough being unable to fly again, the foldiers knock down with long poles.

During

During the flights of thefe pigeons, which crofs this lake into Canada, and are continually flying about in large flocks, the Canadians find great amufement in fhooting them, which they do after a very fingular manner: in the day time they go into the woods, and make ladders by the fide of the tall pines, which the pigeons rooft on, and when it is dark they creep foftly under and fire up this ladder, killing them in great abundance; they then ftrike a light, and firing a knot of the pitch pine, pick up thofe they have killed, and the wounded ones that are unable to fly.--- During the flights of thefe pigeons, which generally laft three weeks or a month, the lower fort of Canadians moftly fubfift on them

Now I am upon this fubject, it reminds me of what *Monfieur Blondeaux* was continually telling me of, *le grand plaifir que j'aurai quand l'été commencera en tuant les tourtes*;

tourtes; adding, at the fame time, with great pleafure, *amufement que le Canadien aime beaucoup*. However, as to the numbers he ufed always to join with this obfervation, I generally thought my good landlord was fetting off his country to great advantage by dealing in the marvellous, and fhould have been impreffed with that idea, had I not been by ocular demonftration convinced to the contrary.

Not only at this encampment, but likewife at our former ones, we were under the neceffity of clearing the thick underwood, and cutting down the fmall trees before we could encamp, during which time you are almoft devoured with the mufquitos, that fwarm in great abundance, and are continually peftering you till the fires are lighted, when the fmoke immediately difperfes them.

T 3   In

In clearing the woods for our encampment at this place, a very favorite dog of Lord Balcarres's, of the Newfoundland breed, had a moſt miraculous eſcape; in the very inſtant that a heavy pine tree was falling, the dog run acroſs, the tree fell, and cruſhed the poor creature into the earth; in this ſituation every aſſiſtance was given, and when he was extricated, he came jumping and friſking up to his maſter, to the ſurprize of every one, who naturally imagined the creature muſt have had all its bones broken, for when the tree fell, it ſhook the earth ſome diſtance round. The preſervation of the dog is entirely attributed to the nature of the ſoil, which was ſandy and pliable. I need not, add, after this event, how much his Lordſhip prizes his favorite dog *Batteaux*.

Two miles up this river there is a ſawmill, and a fall of water, where there is moſt excellent trout-fiſhing. You who

are

are fo fond of the diverfion of angling, would find moft excellent fport in this country. How I could wifh you here, only for an hour, in that employment, that I might have the happinefs, for that little time, of converfing with you, to afk you a thoufand queftions, to hear of thofe who are dear to me, to——but I muft ftop my reflection and my wifhes together.

Yours, &c.

LET-

LETTER XXVII.

Camp at River Bouquet, ⎱ *June* 24, 1777.
  upon Lake Champlain, ⎰

MY DEAR FRIEND,

THIS river derives its name from a Colonel *Bouquet*, who commanded an expedition againſt the Indians, whilſt Canada was under the French Government, as at this place he had a converſation with them upon a treaty of peace.

It ſhould ſeem as if it was the deſtined ſpot to have intercourſe with Indians, for yeſterday General Burgoyne had a conference with them ; and as I am ſenſible how much our employing Indians in this

war

war is reprobated in England, I ſhall give
you the General's ſpeech, and their anſwer,
of which you may form your own opinion.
When the aſſembly were met, the General
thus addreſſed them, by means of an interpreter :

" *Chiefs and Warriors,*

" THE great King, our common father,
" and the patron of all who ſeek and de-
" ſerve his protection, has conſidered with
" ſatisfaction the general conduct of the
" Indian tribes, from the beginning of
" the troubles in America.   Too ſagacious
" and too faithful to be deluded or cor-
" rupted, they have obſerved the violated
" rights of the parental power they love,
" and burned to vindicate them.   A few
" individuals alone, the refuſe of a ſmall
" tribe, at the firſt were led aſtray : and
" the miſrepreſentations, the ſpecious al-
" lurements, the inſidious promiſes, and
                              " diverſified

" diverſified plots in which the rebels are
" exerciſed, and all of which they employed
" for that effect, have ſerved only in the
" end to enhance the honor of the tribes
" in general, by demonſtrating to the
" world how few and how contemptible
" are the apoſtates!   It is a truth known
" to you all, theſe pitiful examples except-
" ed (and they have probably before this
" day hid their faces in ſhame) the collec-
" tive voices and hands of the Indian tribes
" over this vaſt continent, are on the ſide
" of juſtice, of law, and the King.

   " The reſtraint you have put upon your
" reſentment in waiting the King your
" father's call to arms, the hardeſt proof,
" I am perſuaded, to which your affection
" could have been put, is another mani-
" feſt and affecting mark of your adher-
" ence to that principle of connection to
" which you were always fond to allude,
                                             and

" and which is the mutual joy and the
" duty of the parent to cherifh.

" The clemency of your father has been
" abufed, the offers of his mercy have
" been defpifed, and his farther patience
" would, in his eyes, become culpable,
" in as much as it would with-hold re-
" drefs from the moft grievous oppreffions
" in the provinces, that ever difgraced
" the hiftory of mankind. It therefore
" remains for me, the General of one of
" his Majefty's armies, and in this council
" his reprefentative, to releafe you from
" thofe bonds which your obedience im-
" pofed—Warriors you are free—go forth
" in might and valor of your caufe—ftrike
" at the common enemies of Great Britain
" and America—difturbers of public order,
" peace and happinefs, deftroyers of com-
" merce, parricides of ftate."

The

The General then directing their attentions, by pointing to the officers, both German and Britifh, that attended this meeting, proceeded :

" The circle round you, the chiefs of
" his Majefty's European forces, and of
" the Princes his allies, efteem you as
" brothers in the war; emulous in glory
" and in friendfhip, we will endeavor re-
" ciprocally to give and to receive ex-
" amples; we know how to value, and
" we will ftrive to imitate your prefever-
" ance in enterprize and your conftancy,
" to refift hunger, wearinefs and pain.
" Be it our tafk, from the dictates of our
" religion, the laws of our warfare, and
" the principles and intereft of our policy,
" to regulate your paffions when they over-
" bear, to point out where it is nobler to
" fpare than to revenge, to difcriminate
" degrees of guilt, to fufpend the uplifted
" ftroke, to chaftife and not to deftroy.
                                    " This

" This war to you my friends is new;
" upon all former occasions, in taking
" the field, you held yourselves authorized
" to destroy wherever you came, because
" every where you found an enemy. The
" case is now very different.

" The King has many faithful subjects
" dispersed in the provinces, consequently
" you have many brothers there, and these
" people are more to be pitied, that they
" are persecuted or imprisoned wherever
" they are discovered or suspected, and to
" dissemble, to a generous mind, is a yet
" more grievous punishment.

" Persuaded that your magnanimity of
" character, joined to your principles of
" affection to the King, will give me fuller
" controul over your minds, than the mili-
" tary rank with which I am invested. I en-
" join your most serious attention to the
" rules which I hereby proclaim for your
" invariable

" invariable obſervation during the cam-
" paign."

After anſwering, *Etow! Etow!* in their
language ſignifying approbation, they appeared to pay very great attention to the
interpreter, eager to catch the General's
inſtructions.

" I poſitively forbid blood-ſhed, when
" you are not oppoſed in arms.

" Aged men, women, children and pri-
" ſoners, muſt be held ſacred from the
" knife or hatchet, even in the time of
" actual conflict.

" You ſhall receive compenſation for
" the priſoners you take, but you ſhall
" be called to account for ſcalps.

" In conformity and indulgence of your
" cuſtoms, which have affixed an idea of
" honor

" honor to fuch badges of victory, you
" fhall be allowed to take the fcalps of the
" dead, when killed by your fire and in
" fair oppofition; but on no account, or
" pretence, or fubtilty, or prevarication,
" are they to be taken from the wounded,
" or even dying; and ftill lefs pardonable,
" if poffible, will it be held, to kill men in
" that condition, on purpofe, and upon a
" fuppofition that this protection to the
" wounded would be thereby evaded.

Cannot scalp unless dead

  " Bafe, lurking affaffins, incendiaries,
" ravagers and plunderers of the country,
" to whatever army they may belong, fhall
" be treated with lefs referve; but the lati-
" tude muft be given you by order, and I
" muft be the judge on the occafion.

  " Should the enemy, on their parts, dare
" to countenance acts of barbarity towards
" thofe who may fall into their hands, it
" fhall be yours alfo to retaliate: but till
        " this

" this feverity be thus compelled, bear im-
" moveable in your hearts this folid maxim,
" (it cannot be too deeply impreffed) that
" the great effential reward, the worthy
" fervice of your alliance, the fincerity of
" your zeal to the King, your father and
" never-failing protector, will be examined
" and judged upon the teft only of your
" fteady and uniform adherence to the
" orders and counfels of thofe to whom
" his Majefty has entrufted the direction
" and honor of his arms."

After the General had finifhed his fpeech,
they all of them cried out, *Etow! Etow!
Etow!* and after remaining fome little time
in confultation, an old Chief of the *Iroquois* rofe up, and made the following
anfwer :

" I ftand up in the name of all the na-
" tions prefent to affure our father, that
" we have attentively liftened to his dif-
                                " courfe---

" courfe---we receive you as our father,
" becaufe when you fpeak we hear the voice
" of our great father beyond the great lake.

" We rejoice in the approbation you have
" exprefled of our behaviour.

" We have been tried and tempted by
" the Boftonians; but we have loved our
" father, and our hatchets have been
" fharpened upon our affections.

" In proof of the fincerity of our pro-
" feffions, our whole villages, able to go
" to war, are come forth. The old and
" infirm, our infants and wives, alone re-
" main at home.

" With one common affent, we promife
" a conftant obedience to all you have
" ordered, and all you fhall order, and
" may the father of days give you many,
" and fuccefs."

Vol. I.   U   After

After the Chief of the *Iroquois* had finifhed, they all as before cried out, *Etow!* *Etow! Etow!* and the meeting broke up.

One of the General's Aid-de-Camps informed me, that the General was highly pleafed to find the Indians fo tractable, hoping the effential fervice to be expected, would be obtained in employing them. It is through the friendfhip of Captain ****, who took the fpeeches down, that I am enabled to fend them to you.

Orders being given that the army is to embark to-morrow at day-break, to proceed up the lake, and having many things to adjuft, I hope you will pardon my making a hafty conclufion, and remain,

Yours, &c.

An Indian Warrior
Entering his Wigwam with a Scalp.

LETTER XXVIII.

Camp at *Button-Mole-Bay,*} *June* 24, 1777.
upon Lake Champlain,}

MY DEAR FRIEND,

AFTER the meeting of the Indians at river *Bouquet*, the General ordered them some liquor, and they had a war-dance, in which they throw themselves in various postures, every now and then making most hideous yells; as to their appearance, nothing more horrid can you paint to your imagination, being dressed in such an *outre* manner, some with the skins of bulls with the horns upon their heads, others with a great quantity of feathers, and many in a state of total nudity: there

U 2   was

was one among them at whofe modefty I
could not help fmiling, and who, rather
than be divefted of any covering, had tied
a blackbird before him. Joined to thefe
ftrange dreffes, and added to the grotefque
appearance, they paint their faces of various colors, with a view to infpire an additional horror. It is almoft incredible to
think what a prodigious degree of conceit
and foppery reigns amongft the favages in
decorating their perfons, perhaps not inferior to that by which alone fome of our
pretty fellows of the prefent age fo confpi-
cuoufly diftinguifh themfelves. The following ftriking inftance of it, feveral other
officers, as well as myfelf, were eye-witneffes
to, and it afforded us no fmall entertainment:

In our way to their encampment, we
obferved a young Indian who was preparing
for the war-dance, feated under a *wigwam*,
with a fmall looking-glafs placed before
him,

him, and furrounded with feveral papers, filled with different paints. At our ftopping to obferve him, he was at firft a little difconcerted, and appeared difpleafed, but foon after proceeded to adorn himfelf. He firft fmeared his face with a little bear's greafe, then rubbed in fome vermillion, then a little black, blue, and green paints, and having viewed himfelf for fome time in the glafs, in a rage he wiped it all off, and began again, but with no better fuccefs, ftill appearing diffatisfied. We went on to the council, which lafted near two hours, and on our return found the Indian in the fame pofition, and at the fame employment, having nearly confumed all his ftock of colors! What a pity it is the ladies in England, adepts in this art, have not fuch a variety of tints to exercife their genius with!---in my mind, if they muft paint, the more ridiculous they appear, the better.

U 3

Bear's

Bear's greafe, indeed, would not be a very delicate perfume, but no matter——if nature muft be patched up, it little fignifies with what!——I could laugh at the ftreaks on an Indian, but am ftruck with contempt at the airs put on by your flirts, from a penny-worth of carmine, and touched with pity when *fixty* would affume the glow of *fifteen*, through a falfe fhame, or a childifh want of admiration!

An Indian's idea of war confifts in never fighting in an open field, but upon fome very extraordinary occafion, for they confider this method as unworthy an able warrior, and as an affair in which fortune governs, more than prudence or courage.

They are of effential fervice in either defending or invading a country, being extremely fkilful in the art of furprizing, and watching the motions of an enemy.

On

On a fecret expedition they light no fire
to warm themfelves, nor prepare their
victuals, but fubfift merely on the miferable
pittance of fome of their meal mixed
with water; they lie clofe to the ground
all day, and only march in the night;
while halting to reft and refrefh themfelves,
fcouts are fent out on every fide to reconnoitre
the country, and beat up every
place where they fufpect an enemy can lie
concealed. Two of the principal things
that enable them to find out their enemies,
is the fmoke of their fires, which they fmell
at a vaft diftance, and their tracks, in the
difcovery and diftinguifhing of which they
are poffeffed of a fagacity equally aftonifhing, for they will difcern by the footfteps,
that to us would appear extremely con-
fufed, nearly the number of men, and the
length of time fince they paffed; this latter
circumftance was confirmed to me by an
officer, who has the fuperintending of
their tribes. Being out upon a fcout with
them

them, they difcerned fome footfteps, when
the Indians told him that feven or eight
people had paffed that way, and that only
two or three days fince: they had not
gone far, before they came to a plantation
with a houfe upon it, and as is the cuftom
with the Indians, ran up to it, and furprized a fcouting party of the Americans,
confifting of feven, who had come there
the over-night.

In travelling through the woods, they
carefully obferve the trees, efpecially the
tall pines, which are for the moft part void
of foliage, on the branches that are expofed to the north wind, the trunk on that
fide having the bark extremely rugged, by
which they afcertain the direction to be
taken ; and for the more eafy difcovery of
their way back again, their tomahawks are
continually blazing the trees, which is
cutting off a fmall piece of the bark, and

as

as they march along they break down the underwood.

Every Indian is a hunter, and their manner of making war is of the fame nature,
only changing the object, by fkulking, furprizing and killing thofe of their own
fpecies, inftead of the brute creation.

There is an indifputable neceffity of having Indians, where Indians are employed
againft you, unlefs we had men enough of
our own trained up in that fort of military
exercife, as our European difcipline is of
little avail in the woods againft favages.

The reafon of my dwelling fo much on
the fubject of Indians, is becaufe I am fenfible how repugnant it is to the feelings
of an Englifhman to employ them, and
how much their cruelty and barbarity has
been exaggerated.

They

They fight, as thofe oppofed againſt them fight; we muſt uſe the ſame means as our enemies, to be but on an equal footing with them.   I often reflect on that laconic ſpeech a great and gallant officer made to his men, in the laſt war, previous to their going to battle, " there, my brave lads, " there's the enemy, and, by God, if you " do not kill them, they'll kill you."

There is a very great natural curioſity upon Lake *Champlain*; I am led to imagine that it was originally two lakes. About the center of it the land contracts to ſuch a degree, that it appears as if the rock had been ſeparated by an earthquake; the paſſage between what are now two rocks, was but juſt wide enough for our large ſhips to paſs through, and that only with a fair wind, on account of the current.   You'll allow the place to be very juſtly named Split-Rock.

This

This bay, where our prefent encampment is, lies on the fouth fide of the lake, and derives its name from the pebbles, of which great abundance are thrown up on the fhores, the exact form of a buttonmould, and where thofe of wood or horn could not be procured, would be no bad fubftitute.

Juft before we entered this bay, there came on a moft violent and unexpected fquall, occafioned by the land winds blowing from the top of the high mountains on the north fide of the lake; it was but of fhort duration, but very terrible while it lafted.   You will form fome idea how powerful, and with what violence it blows from thefe mountains, from the following circumftance: A fmall brig belonging to the fleet, with very little fail, was in an inftant laid flat on her fide, and the crew were obliged to cut away the mafts, to make her rife again.   The lake was vaftly agitated,

agitated, you may eafily judge how very dangerous it muft have been to the fmall *batteaux*, which are conftructed with flat bottoms, and quite ungovernable when it blows hard. Though the men who rowed the *batteaux* in which I was were continually relieved, it was with much difficulty they could bring her into this bay, their ftrength being almoft exhaufted. However, the whole brigade got fafe, except two *batteaux* that were fwamped juft as they got clofe in fhore, but as it was not out of a man's depth, no lives were loft.

During this ftorm I dreaded much for the fate of the Indians in their birch canoes, whom I thought muft have inevitably been funk; upon reflection, indeed, they did not feem to be in fuch perfonal danger, as both male and female, above the ftate of infancy, are eternally in the water; to the furprize of every one, however, their canoes rofe to every wave, and floated like

a cork,

a cork, which muft be entirely owing to the lightnefs of their conftruction; this lightnefs obliged them to remain fome time upon the lake after we had landed, left the waves fhould dafh their canoes againft the fhore and deftroy them.

I omitted to mention in my laft, that at the mouth of the river *Bouquet* there is a fmall ifland, on which were found feveral young fawns, where the does had fwam acrofs to drop them, as if by a natural inftinct fenfible that the buck would deftroy her young. A foldier of the company, who had been on this ifland, got one, which he prefented to his Captain; it was beautifully marked, and fo young, that it could fcarcely walk; we put it on board the *batteaux*, but during the ftorm it was wafhed overboard, and every effort to fave it proved ineffectual, without hazarding the lives of thofe in the *batteaux*.

Every

Every day, as Addiſon ſays, grows

" Big with the fate of Cato and of Rome."

To-morrow we embark from this place to Crown Point, where our operations commence againſt the enemy. Reſt aſſured I ſhall embrace every opportunity of ſending you the particulars of our proceeding.

Yours, &c.

LET-

LETTER XXIX.

Camp at Crown Point, June 30, 1777.

MY DEAR FRIEND,

WE are now within fight of the enemy, and their watch-boats are continually rowing about, but beyond the reach of cannon fhot. Before I proceed farther, let me juft relate in what manner the army paffed the lake, which was by brigades, generally advancing from feventeen to twenty miles a day, and regulated in fuch a manner, that the fecond brigade fhould take the encampment of the firft, and fo on fucceffively, for each brigade to

fill

fill the ground the other quitted ; the time for departure was always at day-break.

One thing appeared to me very fingular, which I am not philofopher enough to account for ; in failing up the lake, on all the iflands and points of land, the water feemed to feparate the trees from the land, and to pafs in a manner through them, having the appearance of fmall brufh wood, at a very little heighth from the water ; nor do the trees appear to come in contact with the land, till you approach within two or three miles of the object, when they fhow themfelves to be diftinctly joined.

I cannot forbear picturing to your imagination one of the moft pleafing fpectacles I ever beheld. When we were in the wideft part of the lake, whofe beauty and extent I have already defcribed, it was remarkably fine and clear, not a breeze ftirring, ſtirring, when the whole army appeared at one view in ſuch perfeét regularity, as to form the moſt compleat and ſplendid regatta you can poſſibly conceive. A ſight ſo novel and pleaſing, could not fail of fixing the admiration and attention of every one preſent.

In the front, the Indians went with their birch canoes, containing twenty or thirty in each, then the advanced corps in a regular line, with the gun-boats, then followed the Royal George and Inflexible, towing large booms, which are to be thrown acroſs two points of land, with the other brigs and ſloops following; after them the firſt brigade in a regular line, then the Generals Burgoyne, Phillips, and Reideſel in their pinnaces; next to them were the ſecond brigade, followed by the German brigades, and the rear was brought up with the ſutlers and followers of the army. Upon the appearance of ſo formidable a fleet, you may imagine they were not a little difmayed at Ticonderoga, for they were apprized of our advance, as we every day could fee their watch-boats. We had, it is certain, a very ftrong naval force, but yet it might have been greatly in the power of the Americans to have prevented our paffing the lake fo rapidly as we have done, efpecially as there are certain parts of it where a few armed vef-fels might have ftopped us for fome time : but it is an invariable maxim with the Americans, of which there are numberlefs inftances in the laft campaign, never to face an enemy but with very fuperior advantages, and the moft evident figns and profpects of fuccefs.

The army is now affembling in order to commence the fiege, as foon as the artillery ftores arrive from Canada, which are daily expected. People in England, whofe rapidity of ideas keep pace with their good wifhes,

wifhes, little imagine that the diftance from this place to Canada is ninety miles, therefore the time it takes to bring forward ftores is neceffarily confiderable. To the great praife of General Carleton, however, very little delay has yet occurred, for he forwards the ftores very expeditioufly, and however ill-treated many people fuppofe he is, or however he may conceive himfelf fo, in not having the command of this army, after being the commander in the laft campaign, he lets no pique or ill-will divert him from doing all the real fervice in his power to his King and country.

In a former letter I mentioned, that we were to intrench at this place: but however meafures may be concerted with the utmoft judgment and precaution for fucceeding, yet when an army has advanced to the place they are to inveft, the General is often convinced, that neither the defcription of others, nor the delineation of maps

X 2 and

and charts have been fo perfect in every
particular, as not to make fome change in
the intended difpofitions neceffary, which
is exactly our prefent fituation, as orders
are given out for us to embark to-morrow.
What will be the future operations of the
army, after the reduction of Ticonderoga,
it is impoffible to fay, but fome vigorous
meafures, no doubt, are to be purfued, as
an extract from the General's orders will
point out to you. It is generally believed,
however, that the army is to force its way
into Albany. The extract is as follows:

" This army embarks to-morrow to ap-
" proach the enemy. The fervices re-
" quired of this particular expedition, are
" critical and confpicuous. During our
" progrefs occafions may occur, in which
" nor difficulty, nor labor, nor life are to
" be regarded. This army muft not re-
" treat." From the laft fentence, it is a
general and fixed opinion throughout the
whole

whole army, that vigorous exertions are to
be made againſt any oppoſition, however
ſuperior, we may encounter. For ſuch an
expedition the army are in the beſt condition that can be expected or wiſhed, the
troops in the higheſt ſpirits, admirably
diſciplined, and remarkably healthy.

I omitted to mention, that ſhortly after
the conſultation with the Indians at the
river *Bouquet*, the General iſſued out a ma-
nifeſto, which was circulated in the frontiers and province of Connecticut, calculated to ſpread terror among the moſt rebellious, to enforce upon their minds an
impreſſion of fear, of the cruel operations
of ſavages, whom he now could reſtrain,
and their eagerneſs to be let looſe; at the
ſame time, in the moſt expreſſive language,
informing them, that powerful forces were
co-operating, both by ſea and land, to
cruſh this unnatural rebellion; inveighing
ſtrongly on the conduct of the preſent

X 3 Gover-

Governors and Governments here as being the caufe of its continuance, and exhibiting, in the moft lively manner, their injuftice, cruelty, perfecution and tyranny; encouraging thofe whofe difpofition and abilities would affift in redeeming their country from flavery, and re-eftablifhing its former government; offering protection and fecurity to thofe who continued peaceable in their habitations, and denouncing all the calamities and outrages of war to fuch as fhould perfevere in hoftilities. How far it may operate in this part of the continent, I have my fears, as the New-England Provinces are the moft violent in their principles of rebellion.

During our ftay at this place, which has been only three days, the rear of the army is come up, and the magazines and hofpitals are eftablifhed, therefore the operations againft Ticonderoga will immediately commence.

I am

I am truly fenfible how averfe you were to my entering the army, but when once immerged, it would be folly in the extreme to fay, that I wifhed to retract. Although I am not an enthufiaft in religion, ftill you know I ever held in the greateft veneration the fupreme Difpofer of Events, and am not infenfible of his protecting hand, a foldier has many hair-breadth efcapes; but fhould it be the fate of war, and the will of Providence that I fhould fall, I fhall die with the pleafing reflection of having ferved my King and country. If I furvive, you may reft affured of my embracing every opportunity to inform you of my deftiny, and how truly I am,

Yours, &c.

LET-

L E T T E R   XXX.

Camp before Ticonderoga, July 5, 1777.

MY DEAR FRIEND,

WE are now arrived before a place
that is not more talked of this war
than the laſt, on account of the memorable ſiege that then happened, in which that
gallant officer was ſlain, who, could his
immortal ſpirit riſe from its cold manſion,
would no doubt be highly pleaſed to ſee
his offspring, one placed at the head of
naval line, and the other of the army,
advancing the pleaſing taſk of reſtoring
peace to a deluded people, led on by a ſet
of

of factious men, to a moſt unnatural rebellion.

By the ſcouting parties juſt returned we
learn, that there is a brigade which oc-
cupies the old French lines on a height, to
the north of the fort of Ticonderoga; the
lines are in good repair, with ſeveral intrenchments behind them, ſupported by
a block-houſe; they have another poſt at
the ſaw-mills, the foot of the carrying-
place to Lake George, and a block-houſe
upon an eminence above the mills, together
with a block-houſe and hoſpital at the entrance of the lake.

Upon the right of the lines, between
them and the old fort, are two new block-
houſes, and a conſiderable battery cloſe to
the water's edge. But it ſeems the Americans have employed their utmoſt induſtry
where they are in the greateſt force, upon
Mount Independence, which is extremely
lofty

lofty and circular. On the fummit of the mount they have a ftar fort made of pickets, well fupplied with artillery, and a large fquare of barracks within it; that fide of the hill which projects into the lake is well intrenched, and has a ftrong abattis clofe to the water, which is lined with heavy artillery pointing down the lake, flanking the water battery, and fuftained by another about half way up the hill. Fortified as the enemy are, nothing but a regular fiege can difpoffefs them.

There has been a fkirmifh with the Indians and a fmall party of the enemy, who were reconnoitering, in which they were driven back into their lines; the Indians were fo rafh as to purfue them within reach of their cannon, when feveral were killed and wounded. Upon the firing of their artillery, the brigade were ordered under arms, and fhortly after the Indians brought the killed and wounded upon litters,

ters, covered with leaves. It was thought this would have been a check upon them, as the firſt that fell was of their party, but it ſeems rather to ſtimulate their valor.

As our friend M--- was looking through a braſs reflecting teleſcope at the enemy's works, he cried out ſhot, and we had ſcarcely dropt down, before we were covered with duſt. He ſaw them run out the cannon of the embraſure, and what I imagine contributed to their pointing them, was the reflection of the ſun upon the teleſcope. After they had diſcovered our ſituation, they fired ſeveral ſhot, but without doing any miſchief.

A very ſingular circumſtance has occured at this encampment. This morning, a little after day-break, the centinel of the picquet guard ſaw a man in the woods, reading a book, whom the centinel challenged, but being ſo very intent on his ſtudies,

ftudies, he made no reply, when the foldier ran up to, and feized him; upon
waking from his reverie, he told the centinel he was Chaplain to the 47th regiment,
but it being a fufpicious circumftance, he
was detained till the foldier was relieved,
who took him to the Captain of the picquet, from whence he was immediately
.fent to General Frafer's quarters. General
Frafer fuppofing it was a fineffe, for the
47th regiment was ftationed two or three
miles in the rear, and the General thinking himfelf perfectly acquainted with every
clergyman in the army, began to make
feveral enquiries concerning the Ameri-
ricans, at which he was more perplexed,
and ftill perfifted in his firft ftory. What
greatly contributed to thefe miftakes, the
man's appearance was not altogether in his
favor, being in difhabille. General Frafer
not being able to make any thing of him,
fent him with an officer to General Burgoyne, who had no knowledge of him.

To

To clear up the matter, the Colonel of the 47th regiment was fent for, who informed the General that he was the gentleman who had delivered a letter from General Carleton, and had only joined the regiment from Canada the preceding evening. The ftudious gentleman little forefaw to what dangers he had expofed himfelf by his morning ramble, till he was ftopped by the centinel. You will naturally think he had enough to cure him from thefe perambulations in the woods.

About three days fince a great fmoke was obferved towards Lake George, and the fcouts brought in a report, that the enemy had fet fire to the fartheft blockhoufe, had abandoned the faw-mills, and that a confiderable body was advancing from the lines towards a bridge, upon a road which led from the faw-mills to the right of our encampment. A detachment from our corps, fupported by the fecond

brigade

brigade, and fome light artillery, under the command of General Phillips, were then ordered to proceed to Mount Hope, to reconnoitre the enemy's pofition, and to take advantage of any poft they might either abandon or be driven from.

The Indians under the command of Captain Frazer, fupported by his company of markfmen, (which were volunteer companies from each regiment of the Britifh) were directed to make a circuit on the left of our encampment, to cut off the retreat of the enemy to their lines : this defign, however, was fruftrated by the impetuofity of the Indians, who attacked too foon, which enabled the enemy to retire with little lofs. General Phillips took Mount Hope, which cut off the enemy from any communication with Lake George; after which we quitted our former encampment, and occupied this poft, which is now in great force, there being the whole of General

neral Frafer's corps, the firft Britifh brigade, and two brigades of artillery. The
enemy have cannonaded the camp, but
without effect, and continued the fame the
next day, while the army were employed
in getting up the artillery tents, baggage,
and provifions, during which time we never
fired a fingle cannon.

This day Luitenant Twifs, the commanding engineer, was ordered to reconnoitre Sugar-Hill, on the fouth fide of
the communication from Lake George
into Lake Champlain, part of which the
light-infantry had taken poffeffion of laft
night; he reported this hill to have the
entire command of the works and buildings, both at Ticonderoga and Mount Independence, of about 1400 yards from the
former, and 1500 from the latter; that
the ground might be levelled fo as to receive cannon, and that the road to convey
them, though extremely difficult, might be
accom-

accomplifhed in twenty-four hours. This
hill alfo commanded the bridge of communication, and from it they could fee the
exact fituation of their veffels; and what
was another very great advantage, from
the poffeffion of this poft, the enemy,
during the day, could not make any material movement or preparation, without
being difcovered, and even their numbers
counted. Upon this report of Lieutenant
Twifs, it was determined a battery fhould
be raifed on this poft, for light twenty-
four pounders, medium twelves, and eight
inch howitzers, which very arduous undertaking is now carrying on fo rapidly,
that there is little doubt but it will be
compleated and ready to open upon the
enemy to-morrow morning. Great praife
is due to the zeal and activity of General
Phillips, who has the direction of this
operation: he has as expeditioufly conveyed cannon to the fummit of this hill,
as he brought it up in that memorable
battle

battle at Minden, where, it is faid, fuch was his anxioufnefs in expediting the artillery, that he fplit no lefs than fifteen canes in beating the horfes; at which battle he fo gallantly diftinguifhed himfelf, by the management of his artillery, as totally to rout the French.

I am happy to embrace the opportunity of fending this by a futler, who is returning down the lake to St. John's. Be affured you fhall know every event of this important fiege, by the firft conveyance that prefents itfelf. Adieu.

Yours, &c.

LET-

LETTER   XXXI.

Camp at Skenesborough, July 12, 1777.

MY DEAR FRIEND,

NO doubt, after so much as I have repeatedly mentioned to you in my former letters relative to Ticonderoga, and the vigorous defence it was universally supposed the enemy would make, you will be greatly surprized to receive a letter from me, at so great a distance beyond that important post; fully to explain to you the manner of the Americans abandoning it, and our progress to this place, I must proceed a little methodically in my description.

After

After we had gained poffeffion of Sugar-
Hill, on the 5th inftant, that very evening
we obferved the enemy making great fires;
it was then generally thought they were
meditating an attack, or that they were
retreating, which latter circumftance really
was the cafe, for about day-break intelligence was brought to General Frafer, that
the enemy were retiring, when the picquets were ordered to advance, which the
brigades, as foon as they were accoutred,
were to follow.

They were foon ready, and marched
down to the works; when we came to the
bridge of communication, we were obliged
to halt till it was fufficiently repaired for
the troops to pafs, as the enemy, in their
abandoning the works, had deftroyed it,
and had left four men, who were, upon the
approach of our army, to have fired off the
cannon of a large battery that defended it,

and retire as quick as poffible. No doubt this was their intention, as they left their lighted matches clofe to the cannon.

Had thefe men obeyed their inftructions, they would, fituated as our brigade was, have done great mifchief; but, allured by the fweets of plunder and liquor, inftead of obeying their orders, we found them dead drunk by a cafk of Madeira. This battery, however, had, through the folly of an Indian, nearly been productive of fatal confequences to the 9th regiment, for juft at the time it was paffing the bridge, as he was very curious in examining every thing that came in his way, he took up a match that lay on the ground, with fome fire ftill remaining in it, when a fpark dropping upon the priming of a cannon, it went off, loaded with all manner of com-buftibles, but it fortunately happened the gun was fo elevated, no mifchief enfued.

Shortly

In a fhort time after the bridge was rendered paffable, our brigade croffed, and we advanced up to the picqueted fort, where the Britifh colours were inftantly hoifted. The Americans certainly had planned fome fcheme, which proved abortive, and which was left perhaps to the commiffion of thofe men who remained behind, for the ground was ftrewed all over with gunpowder, and there were likewife feveral cafks of it with the tops ftruck out.

After we had remained fome little time in the fort, orders came for the advanced corps to march in purfuit of the enemy, who, we were informed, had gone to Huberton, in order to harrafs their rear. We marched till one o'clock, in a very hot and fultry day, over a continued fucceffion of fteep and woody hills; the diftance I cannot afcertain, but we were marching very

Y 3

expe-

expeditiously from four in the morning to
that time.

On our march we picked up several
stragglers, from whom General Frafer
learnt that the rear-guard of the enemy
was compofed of chofen men, commanded
by a Colonel Francis, who was reckoned
one of their beft officers.

During the time the advanced corps
halted to refrefh, General Reidefel came
up, and after confulting with General
Frafer, and making arrangements for continuing the purfuit, we marched forward
again three miles nearer the enemy, to an
advantageous fituation, where we lay that
night on our arms.

At three in the morning our march was
renewed, and about five we came up with
the enemy, who were bufily employed in
cooking their provifions.

Major

Major Grant, of the 24th regiment, who had the advanced guard, attacked their picquets, which were foon driven in to the main body. From this attack we lament the death of this very gallant and brave officer, who in all probability fell a victim to the great difadvantages we experience peculiar to this unfortunate conteft, thofe of the rifle-men. Upon his coming up with the enemy, he got upon the ftump of a tree to reconnoitre, and had hardly given the men orders to fire, when he was ftruck by a rifle ball, fell off the tree, and never uttered another fyllable.

The light infantry then formed, as well as the 24th regiment, the former of which fuffered very much from the enemy's fire, particularly the companies of the 29th and 34th regiments. The grenadiers were ordered to form to prevent the enemy's getting to the road that leads to Caftle-Town, which they were endeavouring to do, and

Y 4

were

were repulfed, upon which they attempted
their retreat by a very fteep mountain to
Pittsford. The grenadiers fcrambled up
an afcent which appeared almoft inaccef-
fible, and gained the fummit of the mountain before them; this threw them into
great confufion, and that you may form
fome idea how fteep the afcent muft have
been, the men were obliged to fling their
firelocks and climb up the fide, fometimes
refting their feet upon the branch of a
tree, and fometimes on a piece of the rock;
had any been fo unfortunate as to have
miffed his hold, he muft inevitably been
dafhed to pieces.

Although the grenadiers had gain'd the
fummit of this mountain, and the Americans had loft great numbers of their men,
with their brave commander Col. Francis,
ftill they were far fuperior in numbers to
the Britifh, and the conteft remained
doubtful till the arrival of the Germans,
when

when the Americans fled on all fides, whofe
numbers amounted to 2000; they were
oppofed only by 850 Britifh, as it was
near two hours before the Germans made
their appearance.

General Reidefel had come to the field
of action a confiderable time before his
troops, and in the courfe of the action
paffing by him, I could not help feeling
for his fituation, for the honor of a
brave officer, who was pouring forth every
imprecation againft his troops, for their
not arriving at the place of action time
enough to earn the glories of the day.

Upon their arrival, we were apprehen-
five, by the noife we heard, that a reinforcement had been fent back from the main
body of the American army for the fupport of their rear-guard, for they began
finging pfalms on their advance, and at
the fame time kept up an inceffant firing,
which

which totally decided the fate of the day;
but even after the action was over, there
were lurking parties hovering about the
woods.

During the battle the Americans were
guilty of fuch a breach of all military rules,
as could not fail to exafperate our foldiers.
The action was chiefly in woods, interfperfed with a few open fields. Two companies of grenadiers, who were ftationed
in the fkirts of the wood, clofe to one of
thefe fields, to watch that the enemy did
not out-flank the 24th regiment, obferved
a number of the Americans, to the amount
of near fixty, coming acrofs the field, with
their arms clubbed, which is always confidered to be a furrender as prifoners of
war. The grenadiers were reftrained from
firing, commanded to ftand with their
arms, and fhew no intention of hoftility:
when the Americans had got within ten
yards, they in an inftant turned round
their

their mufquets, fired upon the grenadiers, and run as faft as they could into the woods; their fire killed and wounded a great number of men, and thofe who efcaped immediately purfued them, and gave no quarter.

This war is very different to the laft in Germany; in this the life of an individual is fought with as much avidity as the obtaining a victory over an army of thoufands, of which the following is a melancholy inftance:

comparison to other wars.

After the action was over, and all firing had ceafed for near two hours, upon the fummit of the mountain I have already defcribed, which had no ground any where that could command it, a number of officers were collected to read the papers taken out of the pocket book of Colonel Francis, when Captain Shrimpton, of the 62d regiment, who had the papers in his hand, jumped

jumped up and fell, exclaiming, " he was
" feverely wounded;" we all heard the
ball whiz by us, and turning to the place
from whence the report came, faw the
fmoke : as there was every reafon to imagine the piece was fired from fome tree,
a party of men were inftantly detached,
but could find no perfon, the fellow, no
doubt, as foon as he had fired, had flipt
down and made his efcape.

About five o'clock in the afternoon,
the grenadiers were ordered from the fummit of the mountain to join the light infantry and 24th regiment, on an advantageous fituation ; in our cool moments,
in defcending, every one was aftonifhed
how he had ever gained the fummit.—
For my own part, it appeared as if I
fhould never reach the bottom; but my
defcent was greatly retarded by conducting Major Ackland, who was wounded
in the thigh.

In

In this action I found all manual exercife is but an ornament, and the only object of importance it can boaft of was that of loading, firing, and charging with bayonets: as to the former, the foldiers fhould be inftructed in the beft and moft expeditious method. Here I cannot help obferving to you, whether it proceeded from an idea of felf prefervation, or natural inftinct, but the foldiers greatly improved the mode they were taught in, as to expedition, for as foon as they had primed their pieces, and put the cartridge into the barrel, inftead of ramming it down with their rods, they ftruck the butt end of their piece upon the ground, and bringing it to the *prefent*, fired it off. The confufion of a man's ideas during the time of action, brave as he may be, is undoubtedly great; feveral of the men, upon examining their mufkets, after all was over, found five or fix cartridges,

which

which they were positive to the having discharged.

Deferring the remainder of the particulars of this action, with our march to this place, I remain

Yours, &c.

L E T T E R XXXII.

Camp at Skenesborough, July 14, 1777.

MY DEAR FRIEND,

THE confusion of the enemy on their retreat was very great, as they were neither sensible where they fled, nor by whom they were conducted, after Colonel Francis was killed, when they took to the mountains.

Exclusive of 200 men that were killed, and near 600 wounded, many of whom died in endeavouring to get off, the loss on our side has been very inconsiderable. After the action was over, a Colonel with the

the remains of his regiment, to the amount
of 230, came and furrendered himfelf
prifoner.

The advantages of the ground was
wholly on the fide of the Americans, added
to which the woods were fo thick, that
little or no order could be obferved in advancing upon the enemy, it being totally
impoffible to form a regular line ; perfonal
courage and intrepidity was therefore to
fupply the place of military fkill and difcipline.   The native bravery of our coun-
trymen could not be more refolutely difplayed than in this action, nor more effectually exerted.   It was a trial of the activity, ftrength and valor of every man that
fought.   At the commencement of the
action the enemy were every where thrown
into the greateft confufion, but being ral-
lied by that brave officer, Colonel Francis,
whofe death, though an enemy, will ever
be regretted by thofe who can feel for the
lofs

lofs of a gallant and brave man, the fight was renewed with the greateft degree of fiercenefs and obftinacy.   Both parties engaged in feparate detachments unconnected with each other, and the numbers of the enemy empowered them to front flank and rear.   Some of thefe detachments, notwithftanding an inferiority, moft refolutely defended themfelves, and the fate of the day was undecided till the arrival of the Germans, who, though late, came in for a fhare of the glory, in difperfing the enemy in all quarters.

Having given you the particulars of this engagement, permit me, as it is the firft I ever was in, to make my remarks in the time of conflict.

During the action, every apprehenfion and idea of danger forfakes the mind, which becomes more animated and determined the nearer the time of attack approaches.

VOL. I.   Z   Every

Every foldier feels infpired with an impatient ardor, as if he conceived the fate of the
battle would be decided by the level of his
mufquet, or the point of his bayonet:
but the conflict once over, the mind returns to its proper fenfe of feeling, and
deeply muft its fenfibility be wounded,
when the eye glances over the field of
flaughter, where fo many brave fellows,
who a few hours before were in high fpirits
and full of the vigor of life, are laid low in
the duft, and the ear continually pierced
with the deep fighs and groans of the
wounded and dying. Even the joy rifing
in the bofom at the fight of furviving
friends and brother officers, is faddened by
the recollection of thofe who fell. Such,
my dear friend, are the fenfations of the
mind, before and after a battle.

That foldiers have many hair-breadth
efcapes, I am fure was never more fully
verified

verified, than in regard to Lord Balcarres, who commands the light infantry; he had near thirty balls fhot through his jacket and trowfers, and yet only received a fmall graze on the hip. Others were equally as unfortunate, for upon the very firft attack of the light infantry, Lieutenant Haggit received a ball in each of his eyes, and Lieutenant Douglas, of the 29th regiment, as he was carried off the field wounded, received a ball directly through his heart. Thefe extraordinary events may in fome meafure be accounted for, as the leaft refiftance of a mufquet ball will give it a direction almoft incredible: when the Surgeon came to examine the wound of a poor American, it appeared that the ball had entered on his left fide, and having traverfed between the fkin and the back bone, came out on the oppofite fide.

Z 2

When

When General Frafer had pofted the corps in an advantageous ftate of defence, and made fome log works, as he expected we fhould be attacked, his next thoughts were, how to refrefh the men after the fatigues of the day, provifions being unable to be forwarded, on account of the country's being very hilly; a detachment was fent to fhoot fome bullocks that were running in the woods, thefe were diftributed in ratios to the men, which they eat, dreffed upon wood afhes, without either bread or falt.

Juft at this time chance fupplied the officers with a very acceptable, though fingular fubftitute for bread to their beef: an officer who was at Ticonderoga, by way of a joke, fent his brother a great quantity of gingerbread that was taken at that place, which he now diftributed among the officers, and as General Frafer fhared the fame

fame as the men, he fent part of it to him as a prefent.

We laid upon our arms all night, and the next morning fent back the prifoners to Ticonderoga, amounting to near 250. A very fmall detachment could be fpared to guard them, as General Frafer expected the enemy would have reinforcements from the main body of their army, and oppofe his croffing a wide creek, after we had paffed Caftletown. He told the Colonel of the Americans, who had furrendered himfelf, to inform the reft of the prifoners, that if they attempted to efcape, no quarter would be fhewn them, and that thofe who might elude the guard, the Indians would be fent in purfuit of, and fcalp them.

Leaving the fick and wounded under the care of a fubaltern's guard, to protect them from the Indians, or fcouting parties of the enemy, the brigade marched to

Caftle-

Caftletown, where the men were recruited
with fome frefh provifions and a gill of
rum; after this they proceeded on their
march to the creek, to crofs over which
the pioneers were obliged to fell fome
trees; only one man could pafs over at a
time, fo that it was near dark before the
whole of the brigade had croffed, when we
had feven miles to march to this place.

Major Shrimpton, who I told you was
wounded upon the hill, rather than remain
with the wounded at Huberton, preferred
marching with the brigade, and on croffing
this creek, having only one hand to affift
himfelf with, was on the point of flip-
ping in, had not an officer who was behind him caught hold of his cloaths, juft
as he was falling. His wound was through
his fhoulder, and as he could walk, he faid
he would not remain to fall into the enemy's hands, as it was univerfally thought
the fick and wounded muft. Very fortunately,

nately, however, for them, they met with
no moleftation, and three days after were
conveyed in litters to Ticonderoga, as the
road was impaffable for any fort of carriage.

After we had croffed the creek, General
Frafer was perfectly eafy in his mind concerning an attack, which he had been ap-
prehenfive of the whole day, and gave
orders to make the beft of our way to this
encampment, which was through a road
where every ftep we took was nearly up to
the knees. After a march of near thirty
miles, in an exceffive woody and bad
country, every moment in expectation
of being attacked, till we had croffed the
creek, you muft naturally fuppofe we
underwent a moft fevere fatigue, both of
mind and body.

For my own part, I readily own to you,
that the exertions of the day had fo far

Z 4   wearied

wearied me, that drinking heartily of rum and water, I laid down in my bear-fkin and blanket, and did not awake till twelve the next day. But that I may not fatigue you as much as I then felt myfelf, or make you fall afleep, I fhall conclude with fubfcribing myfelf,

Yours, &c.

LET-

L E T T E R   XXXIII.

Camp at Skenesborough, July 14, 1777.

MY DEAR FRIEND,

WE are ftill encamped at this place, waiting the arrival of provifions, *batteaux*, and many other incumbrances, armies in general are but very feldom troubled with, and is a hindrance which that to the fouthward has not to encounter, for whatever want of water carriage they meet with, the navy can always act in co-operation with them.   I mention this, that you may not be furprized at our not making fuch rapid marches, and

over-

over-running the country, as they in all probability will.

The army are all affembled at this place, and in a few days the advanced corps march to Fort Edward. You would like to learn the movements of the other part of the army, after we got poffeffion of Ticonderoga; I was not with them, but you fhall know what I have been able to collect.

After a paffage had been made, with great difficulty, but with much expedition, for the gun-boats and veffels to pafs the bridge of communication, between Ticonderoga and Fort Independence, (which had coft the Americans much labor and expence in conftructing) the main body of the army purfued the enemy by South Bay, within three miles of this place, where they were pofted in a ftockaded fort, with their armed gallies. The firft
brigade

brigade was difembarked with an intention of cutting off the enemy's retreat, but their hafty flight rendered that manœuvre ufelefs. The gun-boats and frigates purfued the armed veffels, and when the enemy arrived at the falls of this place, they made a defence for fome time, after which they blew up three of their veffels, and the other two ftruck.

On the enemy's retreat they fet fire to the fort, dwelling-houfe, faw-mill, iron-works, and all the building on this plantation, deftroyed the *batteaux* and retired to Fort Edward.

An officer who came up at the time of the conflagration, affured me he never faw fo tremendous a fight; for exclufive of the fhipping, building, &c. the trees all up the fide of the hanging rock, had caught fire, as well as at the top of a very lofty hill.

hill.   The element appeared to threaten univerfal deftruction.

The 9th regiment was fent to take poft at Fort Ann, to obferve the motion of the enemy, as well as to diflodge them: but intelligence having been received that they had been greatly reinforced, Colonel Hill fent word to General Burgoyne, that he fhould not retire with his regiment but maintain his ground; the other two regiments of the brigade, with two pieces of artillery, were ordered to fupport them, with General Phillips, who took the command; but a violent ftorm of rain, which lafted the whole day, prevented their getting to their relief fo foon as was intended, which gave the 9th regiment an opportunity of diftingufhing themfelves, in a moft gallant and fignal manner, by repulfing an attack of fix times their number, and the enemy not being able to force

them

them in front, endeavored to turn their flank, which from their great fuperiority was much to be feared; when Colonel Hill thought it neceffary to change his pofition in the very height of the action, which was executed with great fteadinefs and bravery. In this manner the fight was carried on for a confiderable length of time, the Britifh troops maintaining their ground, and the enemy gradually retiring, were at laft totally repulfed, and fled to Fort Edward, fetting fire to Fort Ann, but left a faw-mill and block-houfe ftanding, which was immediately taken poffeffion of by a party of the 9th regiment.

After we had abandoned this block-houfe and faw mills, and proceeded to Fort Edward, the enemy returned and fet fire to it; and as you defire me to fend you a few drawings of fuch things as I might think
beft

beft worth taking a fketch of, I have fent
a reprefentation of the block-houfe and
faw mill, as being a very romantic view.

The 9th regiment have acquired great
honor in this action; though it lafted fo
long, and was fought under fuch difadvantages, they have fuftained very little lofs.
Captain Montgomery (brother-in-law to
Lord Townfhend) a very gallant officer,
was wounded early in the action, and taken prifoner, with the Surgeon, as he was
dreffing his wound, which happened as the
regiment was changing its pofition.

During this action, that pleafant Hiber-
nian acquaintance of ours, M——, of the
fame regiment, was flightly wounded, and
conveyed into the houfe with the reft of
the wounded, which had been attacked,
as part of the regiment had thrown themfelves into it, for better defence during the
action. Our friend M——, in endeavor-
ing

ing to comfort his fellow-fufferers, in a blunt manner, exclaimed, " By heavens, " my good lads, you need not think fo " much of being wounded, for by Jafus " God there's a bullet in the beam."

As to the other part of the army, fome remained behind at Ticonderoga, fome employed in bringing up the *batteaux*, &c. but the whole are now affembled, and collected at this place.

From the various accounts we have been able to collect of the Americans, relative to their abandoning Ticonderoga, it feemed that upon our gaining poffeffion of Sugar-Hill, a poft which they were certainly very negligent and imprudent in not fecuring, they were greatly difmayed, and feeing the preparations we were making to open a battery, which I before obferved had the command of all their works, they called a council of their principal officers, when

when it was pointed out to them by General Sinclair, who commanded the garrison, that their force was very deficient in numbers to man their works, and that it was impoffible to make any effectual defence, obferving to them that places, however ftrong, without a fufficient number of troops, muft furrender, and that in all probability the place would be furrounded in lefs than four and twenty hours. In this fituation of affairs, the General faw the ruin of his army, and it was his opinion that the fort ought to be abandoned to fave the troops; that the baggage and artillery ftores were to be fent to Skenefborough by water, and the troops were to march by land, by the way of Huberton, to. that place. Thefe propofals being fully approved of by the council, was the reafon of their evacuating it that night, and hazarding the undertaking.

General

General Burgoyne forefeeing the great difficulties of conveying even provifions, fetting apart baggage, has iffued out the following orders:

" It is obferved, that the injunction
" given before the army took the field, re-
" lative to the baggage of officers, has not
" been complied with, and that the regi-
" ments in general are incumbered with
" much more baggage than they can pof-
" fibly be fupplied with means of convey-
" ing, when they quit the lake and rivers:
" warning is therefore given again to the
" officers, to convey by the *batteaux* which
" will foon return to Ticonderoga, the
" baggage that is not indifpenfibly necef-
" fary to them, or upon the firft fudden
" movement, it muft inevitably be left on
" the ground. Such gentlemen as ferved
" in America laft war may remember, that
" the officers took up with foldiers tents,

VOL. I.   A a   " and

" and often confined their baggage to a
" knapſack, for months together."

Fortunately for me, my horſe has come
ſafe round the lakes, which will enable me
to keep the little baggage I brought with
me.

The Indians, animated with our ſucceſs, have acquired more confidence and
courage, as great numbers have joined the
army, and are daily continuing ſo to do.

Unexpected orders being juſt given out,
that Captain Gardner departs to-morrow
for England, and having ſeveral more letters to write, I am obliged to leave you.
Adieu.

Yours, &c.

LET-

LETTER XXXIV.

Camp at Skenesborough, July 17, 1777.

MY DEAR FRIEND,

YOU will no doubt be furprized, that in my account of the proceedings of the army, every circumftance of which feems to add glory and conqueft to the Britifh arms, that I never made mention of the favages, in our purfuit of the enemy from Ticonderoga; they could not, in any refpect whatever, be drawn away from the plunder of that place, and I am afraid this is not the only inftance in which the General has found their affiftance little more than a name.

Thofe

Thofe who have the management and conduct of them are, from interefted motives, obliged to indulge them in all their caprices and humors, and, like fpoiled children, are more unreafonable and importunate upon every new indulgence granted them: but there is no remedy; were they left to themfelves, they would be guilty of enormities too horrid to think of, for guilty and innocent, women and infants, would be their common prey.

This is too much the cafe of the lower Canadian Indians, which are the only ones who have joined our army; but we underftand, within two days march, the *Outawas*, and fome remoter nations, are on the road to join us, more brave, and more tractable, who profefs war, and not pillage. They are under the direction of a *Monfieur St. Luc*, and one *Langdale*, both of whom were great partizans of the French laft war; the latter was the perfon who planned and

executed,

executed, with the nations he is now escorting, the defeat of General Braddock.

If thefe Indians correfpond with the character given of them, fome good may be derived from their affiftance; little is to be expected from thofe with the army at prefent, but plundering.

Plundering Indians

As I hinted to you in a former letter, the General's manifefto has not had the defired effect, as intelligence is brought in that the committees are ufing their utmoft endeavors to counteract it, by watching and imprifoning all perfons they fufpect, compelling the people to take arms, to drive their cattle and burn their corn, under the penalty of immediate death; and, forry am I to add, that numbers of well-difpofed perfons to the fuccefs of our arms, have already undergone that fate! Hiftory, I think, cannot furnifh an inftance, where a war was ever carried on with fo much

A a 3   rancor,

rancor, not only with thofe who feem in-clined to oppofe them, but equally to thofe who would remain neuter.

Numbers have joined the army fince we have penetrated into this place, profeffing themfelves loyalifts, wifhing to ferve, fome to the end of the war, fome only the cam-paign, a third part of the number have arms, and till arms arrive for the remain-der, they are employed in clearing the roads and repairing the bridges, in which the Americans are very expert.

We are obliged to wait fome time in our prefent pofition, till the roads are cleared of the trees which the Americans felled after their retreat. You would think it almoft impoffible, but every ten or twelve yards great trees are laid acrofs the road, exclufive of fmaller ones, efpecially when it is confidered what a hafty retreat they made of it. Repairing the bridges is a

work

work of fome labor, added to which, a ftock
of provifions muft be brought up previous
to our marching to Fort Edward. We lie
under many difadvantages in profecuting
this war, from the impediments I have
ftated, and we cannot follow this great military maxim, " in good fuccefs pufh the
" advantage as far as you can."

While this part of the army is thus employed, the remainder are conveying the
gun-boats, *batteaux* and provifion veffels
into Lake George, to fcour that lake, and
fecure the future route of our magazines ;
when that force is ready to move down the
lake, the army will proceed to poffefs Fort
Edward, by which means the enemy, if
they do not abandon Fort George, muft
inevitably be caught, as they will be enclofed by the two armies,. During thefe
movements General Reidefel is to make a
diverfion into Connecticut, and reconnoitre
the country, and by that feint to draw the

A a 4 attention

attention of the Americans to almoft every quarter.

Our fucceffes, no doubt, muft have operated ftrongly on the minds of the enemy, and they will be equally as anxious to adopt meafures for ftopping the progrefs of our army, as to prevent the imminent danger the northern colonies are expofed to.

On Sunday laft a thankfgiving fermon was preached, for the fuccefs of our arms, after which there was a *feu de joie* fired by the whole army, with artillery and fmall arms; the fermon was preached by the clergyman whom I have made mention of, and an exceeding good one it was, for a parifh church, but not in the leaft applicable to the occafion.

By the beft intelligence that can be gained, we are informed, that General Schuyler is at Fort Edward, collecting the militia

from

from the adjacent countries, which, with the remains of their broken army, is to form a fufficient body for making a ſtand at this place. Their fhattered army have ſuffered incredible hardſhips from the want of proviſions, and the neceſſaries to cover them, from the inceſſant rains that have fell of late, as they were compelled to make a week's circuit through the woods, before they could reach Fort Edward, in order to avoid the various ſtrong detachments that we had in different parts, on the Connecticut ſide.

I omitted to mention to you, that your old friend Captain H—, was wounded at the battle of Huberton, early in the action, when the grenadiers formed to ſupport the light infantry. I could not paſs by him as he lay under a tree, where he had ſcrambled upon his hands and knees, to protect him from the ſcattering ſhot, without going up to ſeewhat aſſiſtance could be afforded him, and

and learn if he was severely wounded. You who know his ready turn for wit, will not be surprized to hear, though in extreme agony, that with an arch look, and clapping his hand behind him, he told me, if I wanted to be satisfied, I must ask that, as the ball had entered at his hip, and passed through a certain part adjoining: he is now at Ticonderoga, and, from the last account, is recovering fast.

We march to-morrow, and on our arrival at Fort Edward you may depend upon hearing from,

Yours, &c.

LET-

LETTER XXXV.

Camp at Fort Edward, August 6, 1777.

MY DEAR FRIEND,

WE are arrived at this place, in which it was thought the enemy would have made a ſtand, but upon intelligence of our advancing, they precipitately abandoned it, as they did the garriſon of Ticonderoga. Very fortunately for the garriſon of Fort George, they had paſſed this place about an hour before our arrival; had they been that much later, they muſt have been inevitably cut off.

The

The country between our late encampment at Skeneſborough and this place, was a continuation of woods and creeks, interſperſed with deep moraſſes; and to add to theſe natural impediments, the enemy had very induſtriouſly augmented them, by felling immenſe trees, and various other modes, that it was with the utmoſt pains and fatigue we could work our way through them.   Excluſive of theſe, the watery grounds and marſhes were ſo numerous, that we were under the neceſſity of conſtructing no leſs than forty bridges to paſs them, and over one moraſs there was a bridge of near two miles in length.

In our march through this wilderneſs, as it may with propriety be called, we met with very little difficulty from the Americans.   They ſometimes, when our people were removing the obſtructions we had continually to encounter, would attack them, but as they were only ſtraggling

parties

parties, they were eafily repulfed. The diſtance from our late encampment to this place was fmall, but the many obſtacles the enemy had thrown in our way, made it a matter of aftoniſhment, confidering the laborious march we had undergone, that we ſhould arrive ſo foon.

On our way, we marched acroſs the Pine-plains, which derive their name from an extenfive fpace of level country, on which grows nothing but very lofty pine-trees. On thefe plains we frequently met with the enemy's encampment, and about the center of them, upon fome rifing ground, there were exceeding ftrong works, defended by an immenfe abbatis, where it was thought they would wait our approach. But this pofition was not fuited to the Americans, for if their lines were forced, their rear was an open extent of country. It is a general obfervation, that they never make a ſtand but upon an eminence, almoſt

moſt inacceſſible, and a wood to cover their retreat.

At this encampment the expected In-dians have joined us ; they ſeem to poſſeſs more bravery, and much more humanity, than thoſe who accompanied us acroſs Lake Champlain, as the following little anecdote will convince you :

A few days ſince ſeveral of them fell in with a ſcouting party of the Americans, and after a little ſkirmiſh, the enemy fled to their *batteaux*, and rowed acroſs the river. The Indians fired at, but could not reach them, and being greatly exaſperated at their making their eſcape, perceiving a hog-trough, they put their fire-arms into it, ſtripped and ſwam acroſs the river, puſh-ing the hog-trough before them. The Indians gained the ſhore lower down than the Americans, ſurprized and took them prifoners,

prifoners, and brought them back in the *batteaux* acrofs the river.

One of the Americans, a very brave fellow, was wounded in the fkirmifh, and unable to walk, when the Indians brought him upon their backs for near three miles, with as much care and attention as if he had been one of their own people.

As the Indians approached the camp, we were all apprized of their bringing in fome prifoners, by their fetting up the war hoop; but every one was aftonifhed, and as equally pleafed at their humanity, in beholding an Indian bringing on his back the chief of the party. He was taken before General Frafer, but would give no anfwer to any queftion, and behaved in the moft undaunted manner. The General imagining that by fhewing him attention he might gain fome information from him, ordered him fome refrefhment,

and

and when the Surgeon had examined his wound, told him he muſt immediately undergo an amputation, which being performed, he was requeſted to keep himſelf ſtill and quiet, or a locked jaw would inevitably enſue; to this he replied with great firmneſs, " then I ſhall have the pleaſure " of dying in a good cauſe, that of gaining " independence to the American Colonies." I mention this circumſtance, to ſhew how chearfully ſome of them will ſacrifice their lives in purſuit of this favorite idol. Such was the man's reſtleſs diſpoſition, that he actually died the next morning. This death was generally regretted, as one among the very few who act from principle; had he ſurvived, a different ſtatement of the caſe might have rendered him as ſtrenuous a loyaliſt, as great a hero, as he was a ſtubborn rebel.

To thoſe who have been averſe to our employing Indians, a melancholy inſtance

was

was lately afforded, that will afrefh fharpen their arguments againft the maxim, and as the matter will certainly be greatly exaggerated, when the accounts of it arrive in England, I fhall relate to you the circumftance, as it really happened, and clearly point out the misfortune not to be the effect of their natural barbarity, but a difputed point of war.

A young lady, whofe parents being well affected to Government, had abandoned their habitation to avoid the ill treatment of the Americans, and left their child alone in it, who, upon the approach of our army, was determined to leave her father's houfe and join it, as a young man, to whom fhe was on the point of being married, was an officer in the provincial troops. Some Indians, who were out upon a fcout, by chance met with her in the woods; they at firft treated her with every mark of civility they are capable of, and were conducting her into camp; when within a mile of it, a dispute arose between the two Indians, whose prisoner she was, and words growing very high, one of them, who was fearful of losing the reward for bringing her safe into camp, most inhumanly struck his tomahawk into her skull, and she instantly expired.

The situation of the General, whose humanity was much shocked at such an instance of barbarity, was very distressing and critical; for however inclined he might be to punish the offender, still it was hazarding the revenge of the Indians, whose friendship he had to court, rather than to seek their enmity.

The Chief of the tribe to which the Indian belonged, readily consented to his being delivered up to the General, to act with him as he thought proper; but at the same time said, it was the rules of their

war,

war, that if two of them at the fame inftant feized a prifoner, and feemed to have
an equal claim, in cafe any difpute arofe
between them, they foon decided the conteft, for the unhappy caufe was fure to
become a victim to their contention.

Thus fell a poor unfortunate young
lady, whofe death muft be univerfally
lamented. I am afraid you will accufe
me of great apathy, and conclude the fcenes
of war to have hardened my feelings, when
I fay, that this circumftance, put in competition with all the horrors attendant on
this unfortunate conteft, and which, in all
probability, are likely to increafe hourly, is
but of little moment.

The General fhewed great refentment to
the Indians upon this occafion, and laid
reftraints upon their difpofitions to commit
other enormities. He was the more exaf-

B b 2   perated,

perated, as they were Indians of the remoter tribes who had been guilty of this offence, and whom he had been taught to look upon as more warlike. I believe, however, he has found equal depravity of principle reigns throughout the whole of them, and the only pre-eminence of the remoter tribes confifts in their ferocity.

From this time there was an apparent change in their tempers; their ill humor and mutinous difpofition ftrongly manifefted itfelf, when they found the plunder of the country was controuled; their interpreters, who had a *douceur* in the rapacity, being likewife debarred from thofe emoluments, were profligate enough to promote diffention, defertion and revolt.

In this inftance, however, *Monfieur St. Luc* is to be acquitted of thefe factions, though I believe he was but too fenfible of
their

their pining after the accuftomed horrors, and that they were become as impatient of his controul as of all other: however, thro' the pride and intereft of authority, and at the fame time the affectionate love he bore to his old affociates, he was induced to cover the real caufe under frivolous pretences of complaint.

On the 4th inftant, at the prefling inftance of the above gentleman, a council was called, when, to the General's great aftonifhment, thofe nations he had the direction of, declared their intention of returning home, at the fame time demanding the General to concur with and affift them. This event was extremely embarraffing, as it was giving up part of the force which had been obtained at a great expence to Government, and from whofe affiftance fo much was looked for: on the other hand, if a cordial reconciliation was made with them, it muft be by an indulgence in all

Bb 3 their

their exceſſes of blood and rapine. Nevertheleſs the General was to give an immme-
diate anſwer; he firmly refuſed their propoſal, inſiſted upon their adherence to the
reſtraints that had been eſtabliſhed, and
at the ſame time, in a temperate manner,
repreſented to them their ties of faith, of
generoſity and honor, adding many other
perſuaſive arguments, to encourage them in
continuing their ſervices.

This anſwer ſeemed to have ſome weight
with them, as many of the tribes neareſt
home only begged, that ſome part of them
might be permitted to return to their har-
veſt, which was granted. Some of the remote tribes ſeemed to retract from their
propoſal, profeſſing great zeal for the ſervice.

Notwithſtanding this, to the aſtoniſhment of the General, and every one belonging to the army, the deſertion took
place

place the next day, when they went away by fcores, loaded with fuch plunder as they had collected, and have continued to do fo daily, till fcarce one of thofe that joined us at Skenefborough is left.

It is with great pleafure I acquaint you that Major Ackland is fo far recovered, as to affume his command of the grenadiers; he arrived at the camp yefterday, accompanied by the amiable Lady Harriet, who, in the opening of the campaign, was reftrained, by the pofitive injunction of her hufband, from fharing the fatigue and hazard that was expected before Ticonderoga. But fhe no fooner heard that the Major was wounded, than fhe croffed Lake *Champlain* to join him, determined to follow his fortunes the remainder of the campaign.

That your partner in the connubial ftate, fhould you be induced to change

your

your fituation, may prove as affectionate, and evince as tender an anxiety for your welfare, as Lady Harriet, on all occafions fhews for that of the Major, is the ardent wifh of

Yours, &c.

LET-

LETTER XXXVI.

Camp at Fort Edward, Aug. 8, 1777.

MY DEAR FRIEND,

WE ftill remain at this encampment, till provifions are brought up to enable us to move forward, and notwith-ftanding thefe delays in our convoys and ftores, it will certainly be thought we remain too long for an army whofe bufinefs is to act offenfively, and whofe firft motion, according to the maxims of war, fhould contribute, as foon as poffible, to the execution of the intended expedition.

I know

I know it will be the general obfervation in England, that we ought, after we had penetrated thus far, to have made our way to Albany by rapid marches, it being no more than fifty miles diftant from this place. In this inftance it is to be confidered, how the troops are to pafs two great rivers, the Hudfon and the Mohawk, without *batteaux*; to form a bridge, or water-raft, to convey large bodies at once, even admitting the contrivance of a bridge of rafts to pafs the Hudfon, and truft to chance for the paffage of the Mohawk, or in cafe of a difappointment, recourfe to be had to the fords at *Schenectady*, which are fifteen miles from the mouth of the river, and are fordable, except after heavy rains: removing all thefe impediments, for a rapid march the foldier muft of courfe be exempted from all perfonal incumbrances, and reprefented as juft marching from a parade in England, for nothing can be more repugnant to the ideas of a rapid march,

march, than the load a foldier generally carries during a campaign, confifting of a knapfack, a blanket, a haverfack that contains his provifion, a canteen for water, a hatchet, and a proportion of the equipage belonging to his tent; thefe articles, (and for fuch a march there cannot be lefs than four days provifion) added to his accoutrements, arms, and fixty rounds of ammunition, make an enormous bulk, weighing about fixty pounds. As the Germans muft be included in this rapid march, let me point out the incumbrance they are loaded with, exclufive of what I have already defcribed, efpecially their grenadiers, who have, in addition, a cap with a very heavy brafs front, a fword of an enormous fize, a canteen that cannot hold lefs than a gallon, and their coats very long fkirted. Picture to yourfelf a man in this fituation, and how extremely well calculated he is for a rapid march.

It

It may be urged, that the men might be relieved from a confiderable part of this burthen, and that they might march free from knapfacks and camp equipage, being divefted of which, they might have carried more provifion. Admitting this it would not remedy the evil, it being with great difficulty you can prevail on a common foldier to hufband his provifion, in any exigency whatever. Even in a fettled camp, a young foldier has very fhort fare on the fourth day after he receives his provifion ; and on a march, in bad weather and bad roads, when the weary foot flips back at every ftep, and a curfe is provoked by the enormous weight that retards him, it muft be a very patient veteran, who has experienced much fcarcity and hunger, that is not tempted to throw the whole contents of his haverfack into the mire, inftances of which I faw on feveral of our marches. When they thought they fhould get frefh provi-

fion

fion at the next encampment, and that only
when they were loaded with four days provifion : the foldiers reafon in this manner:
the load is a grievous incumbrance—want
but a little way off—and I have often heard
them exclaim, " Damn the provifions, we
" fhall get more at the next encampment ;
" the General won't let his foldiers ftarve."

Confiftent with the idea of rapidity, it
is neceffary to carry forward more provifion than for bare fuftenance during the
march, or how were the men to fubfift
when they arrived at Albany, where the
Americans will certainly make a ftand ? but
even fuppofing they fhould not, they will
of courfe drive off all the cattle, and deftroy
the corn and corn-mills; this can only be
effected by carts, which could not keep
pace with the army, there being only one
road from Albany for wheel-carriage, and
in many places there are deep and wide
gullies,

gullies, where the bridges are broken, and muft neceffarily be repaired. This road is bounded on one fide by the river, and on the other by perpendicular afcents, covered with wood, where the enemy might not only greatly annoy, but where, in one night, they could throw impediments in our way, that would take nearly the whole of the next day to remove, therefore every idea of conveying more provifion than the men could carry on their backs muft ceafe, as the time and labor in removing thefe obftructions, and making new roads for the carts to pafs, before they could reach the army, would inevitably be the caufe of a famine, or the army muft retreat. All notion of artillery is totally laid afide, as in the prefent ftate of the roads, not the fmalleft ammunition tumbril could be carried with the army.

There are many who may be led away with the ideas of a rapid march, and fay that

that artillery is ufelefs; but they can only form their opinion from the warmth of their wifhes.   It is impoffible to judge, or form an opinion, unlefs upon the fpot, for, fpeaking within compafs, there are not lefs than a dozen ftrong paffes, fetting afide the paffage of the Mohawk; where, if ftrengthened with abbatis, which the Americans are expert in making, as they never encamped a fingle night without throwing up works of this fort in a few hours, five hundred of their militia would ftop, for a time, ten times their number of the braveft troops in the world, who had not artillery to affift them.

Having ftated thefe objections to the principles and practicability of a rapid march, you cannot but be fully convinced how neceffary it is to advance with a fuffi-cient fupply of ftores, both of artillery and provifions; and in order to gain a great

fupply

fupply of the latter, as well as to provide
fome teams and oxen, a detachment is going
to Bennington, to furprize a magazine of
the enemy's, which will enable the army to
proceed without delay, and its Commander
to profecute the object of his expedition.

Certainly the fituation of the General is
extremely trying, however zealoufly he is
inclined, and anxious in compleating the
object of his command. For one hour
that he can devote in contemplating how
to fight his army, he muft allot twenty to
contrive how to feed it! This inconvenience the enemy have not to encounter,
as their army is fpeedily and regularly fupplied with every thing, by means of their
navigable rivers, which communicate from
province to province. An American General has only to teach his men to fight,
(that's a pretty difficult tafk you'll fay) he
is never at a lofs how to feed them.

It

It is, from the various circumſtances I have ſtated, greatly to be wiſhed, that the minds of ſome men were more open to conviction, to form their opinions with the greater liberality of ſentiment.

A few days ſince I went from this to Fort George, relative to ſome artillery ſtores, at which place I had an opportunity of ſeeing Lake George, which, altho' conſiderably ſmaller than Lake *Champlain*, in my opinion exceeds it far in point of beauty and diverſity of ſcene.

About the center of the lake there are two iſlands, on the largeſt of which, called Diamond Iſland, are encamped two companies of the 47th regiment, under the command of Captain Aubrey, for the purpoſe of forwarding the proviſions acroſs the lake. This iſland, as well as the one that is cloſe to it, formerly was ſo over-run with rattle-ſnakes, that perſons when they paſſed the lake feldom or ever ventured on them. A *batteaux* in failing up it, overfet near Diamond Ifland, and among other things it contained feveral hogs, which fwam to the fhore, as did the Canadians who were rowing it up : the latter, in apprehenfion of the rattle-fnakes, climbed up trees for the night, and the next morning obferving a *batteaux*, they hailed the people in it, who took them in and conveyed them to Fort George.

Some time after the man who owned the hogs, being unwilling to lofe them, return- ed down the lake, and with fome comrades ventured a fearch. After traverfing the ifland a confiderable time, they at laft found them, but fo prodigioufly fat, that they could fcarcely move, and in their fearch only met with one rattle-fnake, which greatly furprized them, as the ifland was reported to abound. Their wonder, how ever, was not of long duration, for being
fhort

fhort of provifions, they killed one of the hogs, the ftomach of which was filled with rattle-fnakes, and from this circumftance it was natural to conclude the hogs had devoured them fince their landing.

This was related to me by a perfon on whofe veracity I can depend, and feveral of the inhabitants have informed me fince, that if a hog happens to meet a rattle-fnake, it will immediately attack and devour it.

As I am on the fubject of rattle-fnakes, and this country greatly abounding with them, permit me to defcribe to you thofe reptiles, which I am the better enabled to do, having feen one killed yefterday. It was about a yard long, and about three inches in circumference, in its thickeft part; it had feven rattles at the end of its tail, and according to the number of thefe

rattles,

rattles, its age is afcertained, every year producing an additional one, fixed by a fmall ligament within the other, and being hollow, the quick motion of the tail occafions a noife fo peculiar to itfelf, that I cannot mention any thing fimilar to it. The fcales of thefe rattle-fnakes are of variegated colors, and extremely beautiful, the head is fmall, with a very quick and piercing eye; their flefh, notwithftanding the venom they are poffeffed of, is very delicious, far fuperior to that of an eel, and produces a very rich foup.

The bite of thefe reptiles is certain death, unlefs proper remedies are applied. Providence has been fo attentive to our prefervation (a pretty remark you'll fay this, to come from a foldier, who is contributing daily his affiftance to the deftroying and maiming hundreds), that near to where thefe reptiles refort, there grows a plant, with a large broad leaf, called *plaintain*, which

which being bruifed and applied to the wound, is a fure antidote to the ill effects of its venom. The virtues of this plant were difcovered by a negro in Virginia, for which he obtained his liberty and a penfion for life.

This difcovery, like many others equally furprizing, was the mere effect of chance. This poor negro having been bit by one of thefe fnakes, in the leg, it fwelled in an inftant to fuch a degree, that he was unable to walk; lying down on the grafs in great anguifh, he gathered fome of this plant, and chewing it, applied it to the wound, imagining it would cool the inflammation; this giving him inftant relief, he renewed the application feveral times, and the fwelling abated, fo as to enable him to walk home to his mafter's plantation; after repeating the fame for the fpace of two or three days, he was perfectly recovered.

C c 3 But

But however furrounded I may be with venomous reptiles, the clank of arms, and horrors of war, reft affured that neither diftance, time, nor place, can erafe the idea of friendfhip, nor the fweet thoughts of what is left behind ever be leffened in the breaft of

Yours, &c.

LET-

LETTER XXXVII.

Camp at Batten Kill, August 24, 1777.

MY DEAR FRIEND,

IT is with the utmost concern I tell you
the expedition to Bennington has failed, and great numbers made prisoners:
This no doubt will be a matter of great
exultation to the Americans, and divest
them of those fears they had entertained
of the German troops, especially as they
have been defeated by a set of raw militia.
In this enterprize the General left nothing
for chance to do, but planned every thing
his wisdom could suggest to effect it, and
the project would have answered many

desirable

defirable ends, had the execution of it
proved as fortunate as the plan was judi-
cious.

In fome former letter I laid much ftrefs
againft a rapid movement, and endeavored
to point out to you the total impracticabi-
lity of it.   I need only add another argument to imprefs you fully with the fame
fentiments.   The army could no more
proceed without hofpital ftores, than it
could without provifions, for depend upon
it, the General who carries troops into fire,
without precautions to alleviate the certain
confequences, is fure to alienate their affections,   and damp their ardor ; it is ex-
acting more than human fpirit is able to
fuftain.   It is not neceffary for you to be
accuftomed to fields of battle, to be convinced of truth ; let your mind only reft
for a moment on the objects that prefent
themfelves after an action, and then reflect, there is not a mattrafs for broken
bones,

bones, nor a cordial for agony and faintnefs. Thofe whofe ideas are continually
marching with a much greater rapidity
than ever an army did, fuppofe no oppofition, and no fuffering from wounds.
The many helplefs and in agonies, who
muft be cruelly abandoned (fuppofing the
reft could be prevailed on to abandon thofe
whofe cafe might the next day be their
own) make no confideration with men of
precipitate imagination. I fhall clofe this
fubject with obferving, that in my opinion, a General is refponfible to God and
his country for the armies he conducts,
and that he cannot eafily overlook thefe
objects; however anxious he may be, he
muft be patient till a few hundred beds,
and a proper proportion of medicine and
chirurgical materials, can be brought up
for troops that are to *fight* as well as
march.

In

In order to take advantage of the fuccefs that was expected from the expedition
to Bennington, the army moved to the
eaft fide of Hudfon's river, and on the
14th, a bridge of rafts was conftructed,
over which the advanced corps paffed, and
encamped on the heights at Saratoga.

Whatever was the caufe of the failure
of the expedition to Bennington, of which
many appear, the principal one feems to
have been the delay of the reinforcement
that was fent to fupport the firft detatch-
ment, which was from eight o'clock in
the morning to four o'clock in the afternoon of next day, marching two and
twenty miles; the advanced corps, not only
at the time the Germans were fent, but at
the failure of it, felt themfelves much
hurt, thinking it was a duty they ought
to have been employed on, and it was not
till after its failure, that impreffion was
erafed

erafed from their minds, by being informed they were referved for more important
fervices; for in cafe that expedition had
proved fuccefsful, the advanced corps were
to have pufhed forward to the heights
of Still-Water, and intrenched there
till the army and provifions could have
joined; by this means the whole country
on the weft fide of the river to the banks
of the Mohawk, would have been in our
poffeffion.

A few days after we had encamped at
the heights of Saratoga, the bridge of rafts
was carried away by the torrents occafioned by the late heavy fall of rain, and our
communication cut off from the main
body. If the enemy after the late fucceffes,
in our prefent fituation, had been induced
to attack us, the General would have found
himfelf in a very bad pofition, and unable to take a better, as the advanced
corps could not be fupported by the line;

the

the only means of retreat would have been
under the cover of our artillery, therefore
our corps were recalled, after the action
at Bennington, and were obliged to crofs
the river in boats and fcowls, and take up
our old encampment at this place.

The Mohawk nation, which are called
Sir William Johnfon's Indians, as having
their village near his plantation, and who,
in his life-time, was continually amongft
them, were driven from their village by
the Americans, and have joined our army:
they have come with their *fquaws*, children,
cattle, horfes and fheep, and are encamped
at the creek from whence this place takes
its name; when the army crofs the river,
the *fquaws* and children are to go to Canada, and the men to remain.

Upon their arrival I vifited them at
their encampment, and had an opportunity of obferving the mode they adopt in
training

training up their children. They are in
a manner amphibious; there were feveral
of the men bathing in the creek; and a
number of little children, the eldeft could
not be more that fix years old, and thefe
little creatures had got into the middle of
the creek upon planks, which they paddled along, fometimes fitting, then ftanding on them, and if they overbalance the
plank, and flip off with a dexterity almoft
incredible, they get on it again; as to diving, they will keep a confiderable time
under water, nearly two or three minutes.

The mode of confining their young
infants, is by binding them flat on their
backs to a board, and as they are fwad-
dled up to their head, it makes them refemble living mummies; this method of
binding their young, I am led to imagine,
is the caufe of that perfeĉt fymmetry
among the men. A deformed Indian is
rare to be met with; the women would
be

be equally as perfect, but as they grow
up, they acquire a habit, it being deemed
an ornament, of so turning in the feet, that
their toes almoſt meet; the *ſquaws*, after
the have ſuckled their infants, if they fall
aſleep, lay them on the ground, if not
they hang the board they are ſwaddled to
on the branch of a tree, and ſwing them
till they do; upon a march, they tie
theſe boards, with their infants, on their
backs.

As the river is ſubject to continual torrents and increaſe of water, a bridge of
boats is now conſtructing, to preſerve a
communication with both ſides of the river,
which when compleated, the advanced
corps are to paſs over, and encamp at
Saratoga.

I am interrupted by the cries of ſome
Indians who are ſetting up the war whoop,
on their bringing in priſoners.

When

When they arrive, as they imagine, in hearing of the camp, they fet up the war whoop, as many times as they have number of prifoners. It is difficult to defcribe it to you, and the beft idea that I can convey is, that it confifts in the found of *whoo, whoo, whoop!* which is continued till the breath is almoft exhaufted, and then broke off with a fudden elevation of voice; fome of them modulate it into notes, by placing the hand before the mouth, but both are heard at a great diftance.

Whenever they fcalp, they feize the head of the difabled or dead enemy, and placing one of their feet on the neck, twift their left hand in the hair, by which means they extend the fkin that covers the top of the head, and with the other hand draw their fcalping knife from their breaft, which is always kept in good order, for this cruel purpofe, a few dextrous ftrokes of which takes off the part that is termed the fcalp;

scalp; they are so exceedingly expeditious in doing this, that it scarcely exceeds a minute. If the hair is short, and they have no purchase with their hand, they stoop, and with their teeth strip it off; when they have performed this part of their martial virtue, as soon as time permits, they tie with bark or deer's sinews their speaking trophies of blood in a small hoop, to preserve it from putrefaction, painting part of the scalp and the hoop all round with red. These they preserve as monuments of their prowess, and at the same time as proofs of the vengeance they have inflicted on their enemies.

At one of the Indian encampments, I saw several scalps hanging upon poles, in front of their *wigwams*; one of them had remarkably fine long hair hanging to it. An officer that was with me wanted to purchase it, at which the Indian seemed highly offended, nor would he part with

this

this barbarous trophy, although he was offered fo ftrong a temptation as a bottle of rum.

The appearance of a dead body, you muft allow, is not a pleafing fpectacle, but when fcalped it is fhocking; two, in this fituation, we met with, in our march from Skenefborough to Fort Edward. After fo cruel an operation, you could hardly fup-pofe any one could furvive, but when we took poffeffion of Ticonderoga, we found two poor fellows who lay wounded, that had been fcalped in the fkirmifh the day before the Americans abandoned it, and who are in a fair way of recovery. I have feen a perfon who had been fcalped, and was as hearty as ever, but his hair never grew again.

Should I at any time be unfortunate enough to get wounded, and the Indians come acrofs me, with an intention to fcalp,

it would be my wifh to receive at once a
coup de grace with their tomahawk, which
in moft inftances they mercifully allow.

This inftrument they make great ufe of
in war, for in purfuing an enemy, if they
find it impoffible to come up with them,
they with the utmoft dexterity throw, and
feldom fail ftriking it into the fkull or back
of thofe they purfue, by that means ar-
refting them in flight. The tomahawk is
nothing more than a fmall hatchet, having
either a fharp fpike, or a cup for tobacco,
affixed oppofite to the part that is intended
for cutting, but they are moftly made to
anfwer two purpofes, that of a pipe and a
hatchet. When they purchafe them of the
traders, they take off the wooden handle,
and fubftitute in its ftead a hollow cane
one, which they do in a curious manner.

I make no doubt but it will afford you
great pleafure, knowing how much you
are

are interefted in my welfare, when I inform you that I have had fome promotion, and it is the more fatisfactory to myfelf, as I am not removed out of the advanced corps, it being into the 24th regiment. If I efcape this campaign, either through intereft or purchafe, there are hopes of obtaining a company.   With my beft wifhes for your health and happinefs, I am

Yours, &c.

LETTER XXXVIII.

Camp at Freeman's Farm, Sept. 24, 1777.

MY DEAR FRIEND,

THE bridge of boats was foon conftructed, and thirty days provifion brought up for the whole army. On the 13th inftant, we paffed Hudfon's river, and encamped in the plains of Saratoga, at which place there is a handfome and commodious dwelling-houfe, with outhoufes, an exceeding fine faw and griftmill, and at a fmall diftance a very neat church, with feveral houfes round it, all of which are the property of General Schuyler. This beautiful fpot was quite deferted,

not

not a living creature on it. On the grounds were great quantities of fine wheat, as alſo Indian corn; the former was inſtantly cut down, threſhed, carried to the mill to be ground, and delivered to the men to ſave our proviſions; the latter was cut for forage for the horſes.

Thus a plantation, with large crops of ſeveral ſorts of grain, thriving and beautiful in the morning, was before night reduced to a ſcene of diſtreſs and poverty! What havoc and devaſtation is attendant on war! Your coffee-houſe acquaintance, who fight battles over a bottle of wine, and dictate what armies ſhould do, were danger only to ſhew itſelf upon your coaſt, and threaten an invaſion, would inſtantly, like the poſſeſſors of this delightful ſpot, be flying to the moſt interior parts of the kingdom.

On

On the 15th the whole army made a movement forward, and encamped at a place called *Dovacote*.

I omitted to mention a fad accident that happened to that amiable woman, Lady Harriet Ackland, a little before we paſſed Hudſon's river, which neither has altered her reſolution nor her chearfulneſs, but ſhe continues her progreſs, partaking the fatigues of the advanced corps.

Our ſituation, as being the advanced poſt of the army, was frequently ſo very alert, that we ſeldom ſlept out of our cloaths. In one of theſe ſituations a tent, in which Major Ackland and Lady Harriet were aſleep, ſuddenly caught fire; the Major's orderly ſerjeant, with great danger of ſuffocation, dragged out the firſt perſon he got hold of, which was the Major. It providentially happened, that in the ſame inſtant Lady Harriet, without knowing what

what fhe did, and perhaps not perfectly awake, made her efcape, by creeping under the walls in the back part of the tent, and upon recovering her fenfes, conceive what her feelings muft be, when the firft object fhe beheld was the Major, in the midft of the flames, in fearch of her! The ferjeant again faved him, but the Major's face and body was burnt in a very fevere manner: every thing they had with them in the tent was confumed. This accident was occafioned by a favorite Newfoundland dog, who being very reftlefs, overfet a table on which a candle was burning, (the Major always had a light in his tent during the night, when our fituation required it) and it rolling to the walls of the tent, inftantly fet them on fire.

On the 17th the army renewed their march, repairing a great number of bridges, ·and encamped on a very advantageous ground, at the diftance of about four miles

D d 4   from

from the enemy, who are ſtrongly poſted at Still-Water.

At our laſt encampment a circumſtance occurred, which though trifling in itſelf, marks how provident nature has been to the younger part of the brute creation. It is the cuſtom in camp to picket the horſes in the rear of the tents : in the night I was awaked with a great ruſtling of my tent cords, and a ſqueaking noiſe ; on getting up, I found it was a little colt that my mare had foaled. When we reſumed our march the next day, I was much embar-raſſed what to do with the colt, fearful it would weaken my mare, and render her unable to convey my baggage, but I would not have it deſtroyed ; and, believe me, this little creature, only dropped the night be-fore, though in a journey of ſuch a diſtance as ſeventeen miles, through thick woods and bad roads, was as gay and chearful, when we arrived at our encampment, as if

it

it had been in a meadow, after which, you may be fure, I could not find in my heart to make away with it.

On the 18th, the enemy appeared in force, to obftruct the men who were repairing the bridges, and it was imagined they had a defign of drawing us to action, in a fpot where artillery could not be employed; a fmall lofs was fuftained in fkirmifhing, and the repair of the bridges was effected.

At this encampment a number of men got into a potatoe-field, and whilft gathering them, a fcouting party of the enemy came acrofs and fired on them, killing and wounding near thirty, when they might with eafe have furrounded the whole party, and taken them prifoners. Such cruel and unjuftifiable conduct can have no good tendency, while it ferves greatly to increafe hatred, and a thirft for revenge.

On

On the 19th, the army marched to meet
the enemy, in three divifions ; the German
line flanked the artillery and baggage, purfuing the courfe of the river through the
meadows; the Britifh line marched parallel
to it at fome diftance, through the woods,
forming the center divifion; whilft the
advanced corps, with the grenadiers and
light infantry of the Germans made a large
circuit through the woods, and compofed
the right hand divifion; on our right there
were flanking parties of Indians, Canadians and Provincials.

The fignal guns for all the columns to
advance were fired between one and two
o'clock, and after an hour's march, the
advanced party, confifting of the picquets
of the center column, under the command
of Major Forbes, fell in with a confiderable body of the enemy, pofted in a houfe
and behind fences, which they attacked,
and after much firing, nearly drove in the
body

body of the Americans, but the woods being filled with men, much annoyed the picquets, who were very fortunately fupported by two companies of the 24th regiment, one of which happened to be our company, and a piece of artillery, which General Frafer had detached, on hearing the fire of Major Forbes's party, and we came up juft as the enemy fled.

In this fkirmifh, a bat-man of General Frafer's refcued from the Indians an officer of the Americans, one Captain Van Swearingham, of Colonel Morgan's Virginia rifle-men; they were on the point of ftripping him, which the man prevented, and recovered his pocket-book from them, containing all his papers of confequence and his commiffion. He offered the foldier all his *paper* dollars, and lamented he had no *hard* ones to reward him with.

The

The bat-man brought him up to General Frafer (who now had come up to the two companies he had detached) when he interrogated him concerning the enemy, but could obtain no other anfwer, than that their army was commanded by Generals Gates and Arnold. General Frafer, exceedingly provoked that he could gain no intelligence, told him if he did not immediately inform him as to the exact fituation of the enemy, he would hang him him up directly; the officer, with the moft undaunted firmnefs, replied, " You may, " if you pleafe." The General perceiving he could make nothing of him, rode off, leaving him in the cuftody of Lieutenant Dunbar, of the artillery.

My fervant, juft at this period, arrived with my canteen, which was rather fortunate, as we ftood in need of fome refrefhment after our march through the woods,

woods, and this little fkirmifh. I requefted
Dunbar, with his prifoner, to partake of
it, and fitting down upon a tree, we afked
this Captain a variety of queftions, to
which he always gave evafive anfwers, and
we both obferved he was in great fpirits:
at laft I faid to him, " Captain, do you
" think we fhall have any more work upon
" our hands to day?" to which he replied,
" Yes, yes, you'll have bufinefs enough,
" for there are many hundreds all round
" you now." He had hardly fpoke the
words, than from a wood a little way in
our front there came an exceffive heavy
fire.   Dunbar ran to his guns, faying
A——, you muft take charge of the Captain.   There being only one officer, befides myfelf, with the company, I com-
mitted him to the cuftody of a ferjeant, to
convey him to the houfe where the reft of
the prifoners were, with particular orders,
as the General had defired, that he fhould
not be ill treated; I then haftened to my
company,

company, on joining of which I met a number of the men who were retiring wounded, and by this time the firing of the enemy was fuppreffed by the artillery.

Shortly after this we heard a moft tremendous firing upon our left, where we were attacked in great force, and the very firft fire, your old friend, Lieutenant Don, of the 21ft regiment, received a ball through his heart. I am fure it will never be erafed it from my memory; for when he was wounded, he fprung from the ground, nearly as high as a man. The party that had attacked us were again drove in by our cannon, but the fire raged moft furioufly on our left, and the enemy were marching to turn their right flank, when they met the advanced corps, pofted in a wood, who repulfed them. From that time, which was about three o'clock, till after fun-fet, the enemy, who were continually fupplied with frefh troops,

moft

moſt vigorouſly attacked the Britiſh line:
the ſtreſs lay upon the 20th, 21ſt, and 62d
regiments, moſt part of which were engaged for near four hours, without inter-
miſſion. The grenadiers and 24th regiment, as well as part of the light infantry,
were at times engaged. In the conflict
the advanced corps could only act par-
tially and occaſionally, as it was deemed
unadviſeable to evacuate the heights where
they were advantageouſly poſted.

General Phillips, at a very critical
period, when the Britiſh line was hard
preſſed, by a great ſuperiority of fire,
brought up four pieces of artillery, which
reſtored the action, and gallantly led up
to the 20th regiment, at the utmoſt hazard
of his perſon.

General Reideſel exerted himſelf, brought
up the Germans, and arrived in time to
charge the enemy with great bravery.

Juſt

Juſt as the evening cloſed in, the enemy gave way one all ſides and left us maſters of the field, but darkneſs prevented a purſuit.

The troops lay that night upon their arms, and the next day took a poſition nearly within cannon-ſhot of the enemy; we have fortified our right, and our left extends to the brow of the heights, ſo as to cover the meadows, by the river ſide, where the *batteaux* and hoſpitals are placed. The 47th regiment, with the regiments of *Heſſe Hanau,* are encamped in the meadows, as a farther ſecurity.

The great valor diſplayed by the Britiſh troops encountering many obſtructions, and ſuch a powerful enemy, as, from the account of the priſoners, they had nearly treble our numbers in the field, and the great advantage of receiving inſtant rein-forcements, muſt, in the eyes of thoſe who

who judge impartially, reflect the higheſt honor.

Notwithſtanding the glory of the day remains on our ſide, I am fearful the real advantages reſulting from this hard-fought battle, will reſt on that of the Ameri-cans, our army being ſo much weakened by this engagement, as not to be of ſuffi-cient ſtrength to venture forth and im-prove the victory, which may, in the end, put a ſtop to our intended expedition; the only apparent benefit gained, is that we keep poſſeſſion of the ground where the engagement began.

This ſevere-fought battle, and the con-ſequences reſulting from it, will fully con-firm the arguments I pointed out to you relative to a rapid march. The victory muſt inevitably have been on the ſide of the Americans, without our artillery, and what a wretched ſtate muſt the many brave

VOL. I.   E e   ſoldiers

foldiers be in, without any comfort, or an
hofpital to remove them to!

The courage and obftinacy with which
the Americans fought, were the aftonifhment of every one, and we now become
fully convinced, they are not that contemptible enemy we had hitherto imagined
them, incapable of ftanding a regular engagement, and that they would only fight
behind ftrong and powerful works.

We have loft many brave men, and
among that number is to be lamented
Captain Jones, of the artillery, who was
killed at his brigade of guns. The artillery of the army diftinguifhed themfelves
greatly, but this brigade in particular, the
officers and men ftationed at thofe guns
being all killed and wounded, except Lieutenant Hadden, who had a very narrow
efcape, his cap being fhot away as he was
fpiking up the cannon.

Having

Having juſt received orders to attend a working-party, to throw up a redoubt, I am obliged to defer a further account of this engagement till my next. It will no doubt afford you much pleaſure to hear, that in this ſevere action I have eſcaped unhurt.

Yours, &c.

LET-

L E T T E R   XXXIX.

Camp at Freeman's Farm, Oct. 6, 1777.

MY DEAR FRIEND,

WE have gained little more by our victory than honor, the Americans working with inceffant labor to ftrengthen their left; their right is already unattack- able.   Inftead of a difheartened and flying enemy, we have to encounter a numerous, and, as we lately experienced, a refolute one, equally difpofed to maintain their ground as ourfelves, and commanded by Generals whofe activity leave no advan- tages unimproved.

The

The day after our late engagement, I had as unpleafant a duty as can fall to the lot of an officer, the command of the party fent out to bury the dead and bring in the wounded, and as we encamped on the fpot where the three Britifh regiments had been engaged, they were very numerous. In a former letter I defcribed to you the fenfations both before and after a battle, but in fuch an employment, as this the feelings are roufed to the utmoft pitch. You that are pleafed to compliment me on my humanity, *humanity* will think what I muft have felt, on feeing fifteen, fixteen, and twenty buried in one hole. I however obferved a little more decency than fome parties had done, who left heads, legs and arms above ground. No other diftinction is paid to officer or foldier, than that the officers are put in a hole by themfelves. Our army abounded with young officers, in the fubaltern line, and in the courfe of this unpleafant duty, three of the 20th regiment were interred together,

E e 3   the

the age of the eldeſt not exceeding ſeventeen. This friendly office to the dead, though it greatly affects the feelings, was nothing to the ſcene in bringing in the wounded ; the one were paſt all pain, the other in the moſt excruciating torments, ſending forth dreadful groans.   They had remained out all night, and from the loſs of blood and want of nouriſhment, were upon the point of expiring with faintneſs: ſome of them begged they might lay and die, others again were inſenſible, ſome upon the leaſt movement were put in the moſt horrid tortures, and all had near a mile to be conveyed to the hoſpitals ; others at their laſt gaſp, who for want of our timely aſſiſtance muſt have inevitably expired.   Theſe poor creatures, periſhing with cold and weltering in their blood, diſplayed ſuch a ſcene, it muſt be a heart of adamant that could not be affected at it, even to a degree of weakneſs.

In

In the courfe of the laft action, Lieutenant Hervey, of the 62d, a youth of fixteen, and nephew to the Adjutant-General of the fame name, received feveral wounds, and was repeatedly ordered off the field by Colonel Anftruther; but his heroic ardor would not allow him to quit the battle, while he could ftand and fee his brave lads fighting befide him. A ball ftriking one of his legs, his removal became abfolutely neceffary, and while they were conveying him away, another wounded him mortally. In this fituation the Surgeon recommended him to take a powerful dofe of opium, to avoid a feven or eight hours life of moft exquifite torture: this he immediately confented to, and when the Colonel entered the tent with Major Harnage, who were both wounded, they afked whether he had any affairs they could fettle for him? his reply was, " that being a minor, every " thing was already adjufted;" but he had one requeft, which he had juft life enough

to utter, " Tell my uncle I died like a fol-
" dier!"   Where will you find in ancient
Rome heroifm fuperior!

Beyond the ground where we defeated
our enemy, all is hoftile and dangerous in
an alarming degree; it fhould feem as if we
had conquered only to preferve our reputation, for we have reaped little advantage
from our invincible efforts; the only fatisfaction refulting on our part is, the confcioufnefs of having acquitted ourfelves
like men, with a determination that the
honor and renown of the Britifh arms
fhould remain unfullied.   The nature of
the country is peculiarly unfavorable in refpect to military operations, it being difficult to reconnoitre the enemy, and to obtain any intelligence to be relied on: the
roads, the fituation of the enemy, the
grounds for procuring forage, of which
the army is in great want, and all parties
are in queft of, are often attended with the

utmoft

utmoſt danger, and require great bodies to cover them.

The expectation of plunder which had induced the Indians that remained to accompany us thus far, beginning now to fail, and ſeeing they have nothing but hardſhips and warfare, they are daily decreaſing. They were of vaſt ſervice in foraging and ſcouting parties, it being ſuited to their manner; they will not ſtand a regular engagement, either through the motives I formerly aſſigned, or from fear, but I am led to imagine the latter is the caſe, from the obſervation I have made of them in our late encounter with the enemy. The Indians were running from wood to wood, and juſt as our regiment had formed in the ſkirts of one, ſeveral of them came up, and by their ſigns were converſing about the ſevere fire on our right. Soon after the enemy attacked us, and the very firſt fire the Indians run off through the wood.

As

As to the Canadians, little was to be depended on their adherence, being eafily difpirited, with an inclination to quit as foon as there was an appearance of danger; nor was the fidelity of the Provincials to be relied on who had joined our army, as they withdrew on perceiving the refiftance of the Americans would be more formidable than had been expected.

The defertion of the Indians, Canadians, and Provincials, at a time when their fervices were moft required, was exceedingly mortifying; and however it may prove, this inftance, will fhew future commanders what little dependence is to be placed on fuch auxiliaries.

You will readily allow that it is the higheft teft of affection in a woman, to fhare · with her hufband the toils and hardfhips of the campaign, efpecially fuch an one as the prefent. What a trial of

fortitude

fortitude the late action muſt have been, through a diſtreſſing interval of long ſuſpence! The ladies followed the route of the artillery and baggage, and when the action began, the Baroneſs Reideſel, Lady Harriet Ackland, and the wives of Major Harnage and Lieutenant Reynell, of the 62d regiment, entered a ſmall uninhabited hut, but when the action became general and bloody, the Surgeons took poſſeſſion of it, being the moſt convenient for the firſt care of the wounded; in this ſituation were theſe ladies four hours together, when the comfort they afforded each other was broke in upon, by Major Harnage being brought in to the Surgeons deeply wounded! What a blow muſt the next intelligence be, that informed them Lieutenant Reynell was killed! Madame de Reideſel and Lady Harriet could afford but little conſolation to their companions, through an anxiouſneſs they knew ñot how to ſmother, leſt it might be ſoon,

very

very foon, their own fituation. The fears of Lady Harriet were doubly increafed, having every apprehenfion, not only for her hufband but her brother.

Surrounded by the dead and the dying for four long hours, the groans of the wounded, the difcharge of the mufquetry, and all the buftle of arms—my God!— what a ftate for women of fufceptibility! —uncertain how the battle would terminate, and whether each fhould clafp again the object of her deareft hopes, for whofe fake fhe had traverfed dreary regions, encountered hunger and wearinefs, and witneffed all the carnage of a long-difputed field—unanimated by the tumult, and without fharing the glory.

A long war teaches the moft unwarlike nation the ufe of arms, and very frequently puts them in a condition to repair in the end, the loffes they fuftained in the beginning.

beginning. Such is the prefent ftate of
the enemy, who not only now, but before
the late action, were ftrongly recruited.
as powerful armies of militia fpring up in
every province. What a ftriking advantage there was on the fide of the Americans, in the laft engagement; but the de-
fect of numbers in our little army, was
amply made up by the courage of the
foldiers, the valor and conduct of our
Generals.

The officers who have been killed and
wounded in the late action, are much
greater in proportion than that of the
foldiers, which muft be attributed to the
great execution of the rifle-men, who
directed their fire againft them in particular; in every interval of fmoke, they
were fure to take off fome, as the rifle-men
had pofted themfelves in high trees. Some
of the prifoners who were taken late in
the day, faid, it was firmly believed in the
enemy's

enemy's camp, that General Burgoyne was killed, which miftake was occafioned by an Aid-de-Camp of General Phillips, a Captain Green, who, having the furniture to his faddle laced and embroidered, and being wounded, fell from his horfe, the rifle-man that wounded him, from that circumftance, affirmed it to be General Burgoyne.

You would be led to imagine, that the Indians and Canadians would have been of great utility againft this mode of fighting, but the few who remained of the former, could not be brought within found of a rifle-fhot; and the latter, who formerly were very expert in this fervice, either from a great change in their military character, or a damp that was thrown upon them by the lofs of their beft officers, who were under the neceffity of expofing themfelves more than was requifite, in order to bring them at all into action, were of little ufe.

Some

Some of the Provincial troops were serviceable, but the only men we had really to oppose them were the German chaffeurs, but their number was very inferior to the rifle-men of the enemy.

Our present situation is far from being an inactive one, the armies being so near, that not a night passes but there is firing, and continual attacks upon the advanced picquets, especially those of the Germans. It seems to be the plan of the enemy to harrass us by constant attacks, which they are enabled to do, without fatiguing their army, from the great superiority of their numbers.

We are now become so habituated to fire, that the soldiers seem to be indifferent to it, and eat and sleep when it is very near them; the officers rest in their cloaths, and the field officers are up frequently in the night. The enemy, in front of our quarter

ter

ter-guard, within hearing, are cutting trees
and making works, and when I have had
this guard, I have been vifited by moft of
the field officers, to liften to them. You
would fcarcely believe it, but the enemy
had the affurance to bring down a fmall
piece of cannon, to fire as their morning
gun, fo near to our quarter-guard, that the
wadding rebounded againft the works.

We have within thefe few evenings, exclufive of other alarms, been under arms
moft of the night, as there has been a great
noife, like the howling of dogs, upon the
right of our encampment; it was imagined the enemy fet it up to deceive us, while
they were meditating fome attack. The two
firft nights this noife was heard, General
Frafer thought it to have been the dogs
belonging to the officers, and an order was
given for the dogs to be confined within
the tents; any that were feen running
about, the Prevoft had orders to hang them.
The

The next night the noife was much greater, when a detachment of Canadians and Provincials were fent out to reconnoitre, and it proved to have arifen from large droves of wolves that came after the dead bodies: they were fimilar to a pack of hounds, for one fetting up a cry, they all joined, and when they approached a corpfe, their noife was hideous till they had fcratched it up.

I have fent you a view of the encampment of our hofpital tents, park of artillery, &c. from a redoubt we have on the oppofite fide of the river, by which you may be able to form fome idea of the country we are at prefent encamped on. This view was taken by Sir Francis Clerke, one of General Burgoyne's Aid-de-Camps, who has favored me with a copy.

Yours, &c.

LETTER XL.

Cambridge, in New England, Nov. 10, 1777.

MY DEAR FRIEND,

THE difpatches fent by Lord Peterfham, relative to our misfortunes,
will have reached England long before this
comes to hand.   Your furprize, then, will
ceafe at receiving a letter dated from this
place.   As every little circumftance relative
to a campaign, cannot be given in an
official account to be laid before the public,
I fhall relate the tranfactions of the army
till the convention took place.

The

pag 102

Burgoyne reconnoitre

The day after the date of my laſt letter, a detachment of 1500 regular troops, with two twelve-pounders, two howitzers, and ſix ſix-pounders, went out between eleven and twelve o'clock.   The reaſon, no doubt, for the General's marching at this time, rather than earlier in the morning, was, that in caſe we ſhould not prove victorious, he had the night to favor his retreat.

The intention of this detachment was to make a movement to the enemy's left, not only to diſcover whether there was a poſſibility of forcing a paſſage, if neceſſary to advance, or diſlodge the enemy, in order to favor a retreat, but likewiſe to cover the forage of the army, through the ſcarcity of which we were in great diſtreſs.   This *look for food* being a project of much importance, General Burgoyne took with him Generals Phillips, Reideſel and Fraſer, as officers beſt qualified, and with whoſe aſſiſtance he had every hope the plan would ſucceed.

The

The guard of the camp upon the heights was left to the command of Brigadier Generals Hamilton and Specht, and the redoubts and plain to Brigadier General Gall.

This day having the quarter-guard of the regiment, I of courfe remained in camp, and therefore can give you no information as to the various pofitions that were taken; after the detachment had been out fome time, we heard a very heavy firing with the artillery, and fome little fkirmifhing with fmall arms.

At this time Major Campbell, of the 29th regiment, the Field-officer of the day, came to my guard, and defired me to go with a ferjeant and fome men, to reconnoitre acrofs two ravines, in front of the guard, to liften if I could hear the enemy marching that way; all was quiet in that quarter, but as the firing began to be very heavy

heavy on the left, I returned to the guard. In this little circuit I was convinced how much the Americans were pufhed in our late action, on the 19th of September, for I met with feveral dead bodies belonging to the enemy, and amongft them were laying clofe to each other, two men and a woman, the latter of whom had her arms extended, and her hands grafping cartridges.

Soon after my return to the guard, the firing appeared to become general on both fides, and very heavy indeed. Much about this time the bat-men of the army, who went out for forage, came galloping into camp, having thrown off their forage to fave their own horfes and themfelves by flight. The gallant behaviour of an old foldier, of the 20th regiment, deferves to be remembered; he had been wounded at the battle of Minden, and as he lay on the ground a French dragoon rode over him,

F f 3 and

and the horfe's feet refted on his breaft;
after having recovered from this accident,
he thought himfelf invulnerable, and held
the Americans in great contempt: when
they attacked the foraging party, the hardy
old veteran, fitting upon the forage which
he had got on the horfe, kept loading and firing his piece at the enemy, and
in this manner he brought his forage into
camp. Upon his arrival, his mafter re-
primanded him for the danger he had
expofed both, himfelf and his horfes to,
(when he faid) " May it pleafe your honor,
" I could not throw away my forage, I'd
" fooner lofe my life, than my poor horfes
" fhould ftarve."

You muft allow this defeat of the bat-
men, and a number of wounded men
coming into camp, was no very favorable
omen of fuccefs; nor can you conceive the
forrow vifible on General Frafer's being
brought

brought in wounded, your old friends
Campbell and Johnston, of our regiment,
on each fide of his horfe, fupporting him.
I cannot defcribe to you the fcene ; it was
fuch that the imagination muft help to
paint.——The officers, all anxious and
eagerly enquiring as to his wound—the
down-caft look and melancholy that was
vifible to every one, as to his fituation, and
all the anfwer he could make to the many
enquiries, was a fhake of his head, expreffive that it was all over with him.—
So much was he beloved, that not only
officers and foldiers, but all the women
flocked round, folicitous for his fate.

When he had reached his tent, and was
recovered a little from the faintnefs occafioned by lofs of blood, he told thofe
around him, that he faw the man who
fhot him, he was a rifle-man, and up in
a tree; the ball entered a little below his

F f 4   breaft,

breaſt, and penetrated juſt below the back bone. After the Surgeon had dreſſed his wound, he ſaid to him very compoſedly, " Tell me, Sone, to the, beſt " of your ſkill and judgment, if you " think my wound is mortal." When he replied, " I am ſorry, Sir, to inform you, " that it is, and that you cannot poſſibly " live four and twenty hours." He then called for pen and ink, and after making his will, and diſtributing a few little tokens of regard to the officers of his ſuite, deſired that he might be removed to the general hoſpital.

In camp, and not in perſonal danger, as the mind is left to reflection, it is impoſſible to deſcribe how much it is affected in beholding the wounded continually coming in, amid an inceſſant roar of cannon and muſquetry, where perhaps many brave fellows are dying for their country—perhaps

too

too in an unfuccefsful battle! I can never confent to be left in camp again.

After many hours impatient anxiety, towards the clofe of the evening, the grand ftroke came. I had little hope to become a partaker in the action; but about that time the troops came pouring into camp as faft as they could, and fhortly after Generals Burgoyne, Phillips and Reidefel. It is impoffible to defcribe the anxioufnefs depicted in the countenance of General Burgoyne, who immediately rode up to the quarter-guards, and when he came to that of our regiment, I was acrofs a ravine, pofting a ferjeant's guard. Upon enquiring eagerly for the officer, I came to him, " Sir, faid the General, you muft defend " this poft to the very laft man." You may eafily conceive, upon receiving thofe orders, I judged every thing to be in a dangerous fituation. There was not a moment for thought, for the Americans

ftormed

ftormed with great fury the poft of the light-infantry, under the command of Lord Balcarres, rufhing clofe to the lines, under a fevere fire of grape-fhot and fmall arms. This poft was defended with great fpirit, and the enemy, led on by General Arnold, as gallantly affaulted the works; but on the General's being wounded, the enemy were repulfed, which was not till after dark. In this attack, I was but an obferver, as our quarter-guard was fome diftance from the lines, but not fufficiently fo as to be out of danger, as the balls were continually dropping down amongft us. In order that you may form fome idea with what obftinacy the enemy affaulted the lines, from the commencement, at which time it was dark, till they were repulfed, there was a continual fheet of fire along the lines, and in this attack we were fully convinced of what effential fervice our artillery was.

During

During the time the enemy were fo vigoroufly attacking our lines, a party affaulted thofe of the Germans, commanded by Colonel Breyman, but either for want of courage, or prefence of mind, they, upon the firft attack of the enemy, were ftruck with fuch a terror, that inftead of gallantly fuftaining their lines, they looked on all as loft, and after firing one volley, haftily abandoned them; that brave officer, Colonel Breyman, in endeavouring to rally his foldiers, was unfortunately killed. By the enemy's obtaining poffeffion of the German lines, they gained an opening upon our right and rear.

In this engagement we loft many brave officers, to add to the fate of General Frafer, General Burgoyne's, Aid-de-Camp, Sir Francis Clerke, was killed, Colonel Ackland wounded and a prifoner, Major Williams, Captain Blomfield, and Lieutenant Howarth, of the artillery, were likewife

likewife prifoners, the latter wounded; Major Blomfield's wound was very remarkable, a fhot paffing through both cheeks, without hurting the infide of his mouth. Your friend Howarth's wound I hear, is in his knee; it is very fingular, but he was prepoffeffed with an idea of being wounded, for when the orders came for the detachment's going out, he was playing picquet with me, and after reading the orders, and that his brigade of guns were to go, he faid to me, " God blefs you " A——, farewell, for I know not how it " is, but I have ftrange *prefentiment* that I " fhall either be killed or wounded." I was rather furprized at fuch an expreffion, as he is of a gay and chearful difpofition, and cannot but fay, that during the little time I could beftow in reflection that day, I continually dwelt upon his remark, but he is now happily in a fair way of recovery.

After

After Major Ackland was wounded, when he obferved the army were retreating, he requefted Captain Simpfon, of the 31ſt regiment, who was an intimate friend, to help him into camp, upon which, being a very ftout man, he conveyed the Major on his back a confiderable way, when the enemy purfuing fo rapidly, he was obliged to leave him behind to fave himfelf. As the Major lay on the ground, he cried out to the men who were running by him, that he would give fifty guineas to any foldier who would convey him into camp. A ftout grenadier inftantly took him on his back, and was haftening into camp, when they were overtaken by the enemy and made prifoners. Here you muft naturally conceive what were the feelings of Lady Harriet, who, after hearing the whole of the action, at laft received the fhock of her individual misfortune, mixed with the general calamity of the defeat.

Whatever

Whatever favorable opinion the General had entertained of our late encampment, after this attack he thought our flank liable to be turned, and it would be impoffible to accomplifh an honorable retreat, fearing the only fecurity of the army would con- fift in an ignominious flight, as our works would by no means refift cannon-fhot. Before we quitted them, we heard the enemy bringing up their artillery, no doubt with a view to attack us at day- break; therefore, laboring under thefe apparent difadvantages, we had orders to quit our prefent fituation during the night, and take poft upon the heights, above the hofpital; by this movement the whole of the army were now affembled upon the heights and plain, of which you have a view in the drawing I fent you.

Our late movement, which was effect- ed without any lofs, occafioned the enemy to make a new difpofition, and on the

the 8th of October, the baggage and
incumbrances of the army being removed,
we offered battle, anxious for a conflict
in a plain, where we could difcern our
enemy, as hitherto all our actions had been
in the woods, where it is impoffible exactly
to prefcribe to an army, or feparate body,
how to govern itfelf; every different motion of the enemy, and the various accounts a General receives of them, ought
to make him alter his meafures, and there
is no laying down to a commanding officer of any corps, other than general rules,
the reft depending on his own conduct,
and the behaviour of his troops.

At one time we fully imagined it was
the intention of the enemy to have attacked us, as a very large body, confifting
of feveral brigades, drew up in line of
battle, with artillery; and began to can-
nonade us. In return, an howitzer was
fired, and, as was intended, the fhell fell
fhort,

fhort, upon which the enemy fetting up a great fhout, were very much encouraged, and kept on cannonading. The next time the howitzer was fo elevated, that the fhell fell into the very center of a large column, and immediately burft, which fo difmayed them, that they fled off into the woods, and fhewed no other intentions of an attack; indeed their cautious conduct during the whole day ftrongly marked a difinclination to a general action.

Early on this morning General Frafer breathed his laft, and at his particular requeft, was buried, without any parade, in the great redoubt, by the foldiers of his own corps. About fun-fet, the corpfe was carried up the hill; the proceffion was in view of both armies; as it paffed by Generals Burgoyne, Phillips and Reidefel, they were ftruck at the plain fimplicity of the parade, being only attended by the officers of his fuite; but left the army,

not

not being acquainted with the privacy that was defired, and conftrue it into neglect, and urged by a natural wifh to pay the laft honors to him, in the eyes of the whole army, they joined the proceffion.

The enemy, with an inhumanity peculiar to Americans, cannonaded the proceffion as it paffed, and during the fervice over the grave.   The account given me by your friend Lieut. Freeman was, that there appeared an expreffive mixture of fenfibility and indignation upon every countenance— the fcene muft have been affecting.

In the evening intelligence was brought that the enemy were marching to turn our right; we could prevent this by no other means than retreating towards Saratoga. A retreat is a matter of the higheft confequence, and requires the greateft conduct in a General, as well as refolution in both officers and foldiers, for the leaft mifma-

nagement puts all into confusion. A good
retreat is looked on as the *chef d'œuvre* of
a Commander. Every one of the advanced
corps felt severely the loss of General
Frafer, as he used frequently to say, that
if the army had the misfortune to retreat,
he would ensure, with the advanced corps,
to bring it off in safety ; this was a piece
of Generalship he was not a little vain
of, for during the war in Germany, he
made good his retreat with five hundred
chasseurs, in sight of the French army.
But as covering the retreat of the army
was of the utmost consequence, General
Phillips took the command of the rear-
guard, which consisted of the advanced
corps.

At nine o'clock at night the army began
to move, General Reidesel commanding
the van-guard. Our retreat was made
within musquet-shot of the enemy, and
though greatly encumbered with baggage,
                                    without

without a fingle lofs. It was near eleven o'clock before the rear-guard marched, and for near an hour, we every moment expected to be attacked, for the enemy had formed on the fame fpot as in the morning; we could difcern this by the lanterns that the officers had in their hands, and their riding about in the front of their line, but though the Americans put their army in motion that night, they did not purfue us, in our retreat, till late the next day. Deferring the fequel of our misfortunes till another opportunity, and willing to embrace a very favorable one that now prefents itfelf of fending this, I remain,

Yours, &c.

LET-

LETTER   XLI.

Cambridge, in New England Nov. 15, 1777.

MY DEAR FRIEND,

AFTER a march, in which we were liable to be attacked in front, flank and rear, the army, on the 9th, at day-break, reached an advantageous ground, and took a pofition very defirable to have received the enemy ; we halted to re-frefh the troops, and to give time for the *batteaux* to come abreaft of the army. A few days provifion was delivered out, and it was apprehended it might be the laft, for though the movement of the army kept pace with the *batteaux*, ftill there were

many

many parts of the river where they might have been attacked to great advantage, and where the army could afford them little protection.

After the troops had been refreſhed, and the *batteaux* came up, the army proceeded forward, in very ſevere weather, and thro' exceeding bad roads, and late at night arrived at Saratoga, in ſuch a ſtate of fatigue, that the men had not ſtrength or inclination to cut wood and make fires, but rather ſought ſleep in their wet cloaths and on the wet ground, under a heavy rain that ſtill continued, and which began to fall when we firſt retreated.

The inceſſant rain during our retreat was rather a favorable circumſtance, for though it impeded the army in their march, and increaſed its difficulties, it ſerved at the ſame time to retard, and in a great meaſure prevented, the purſuit of the enemy;

it

it however occafioned one very unhappy neceffity, that of abandoning our hofpitals with the fick and wounded: but great praife is due to the humanity of General Gates, for upon the very firft intelligence of it, he immediately fent forward a few light horfe, to protect them from infult and plunder.

The heavy rain afforded another confolation to the men during the march, which was, in cafe the enemy had attacked us, the fate of the day would have refted folely upon the bayonet: this idea prevailed fo ftrongly in the minds of the men, that notwithftanding they were acquainted with the fuperiority of the enemy, an attack feemed to be the wifh of every foldier.

When the army were about to move after we halted, the cares and anxieties with which the General, no doubt, muft have been furrounded, were greatly increafed

creafed by a circumftance of private diftrefs, for at this time a meffage was delivered to him from that amiable woman, Lady Harriet Ackland, expreffing an earneft defire, if it did not militate againft the General's wifhes, of paffing to the camp of the enemy, and requefting General Gates's permiffion to attend her hufband, at the fame time fubmitting it entirely to the General's opinion.

The General, although he had been fully convinced of the patience and fortitude with which fhe had already encountered the many trying fituations that had befallen her, could not but exprefs his aftonifhment at this propofal, as it appeared an effort beyond human nature, that a woman of fuch a tender and delicate frame as her's, fhould be capable of fuch an undertaking as that of delivering herfelf to the enemy—probaby in the night, and uncertain of what hands fhe might fall into—

G g 4   efpecially

efpecially after fo long an agitation of the
fpirits, not only exhaufted by want of reft,
but abfolutely want of food, and drenched
in rains for near twelve hours—and this at
a time too, when far advanced in a ftate
where every tender care and precaution becomes abfolutely requifite!——In the harraffed and fatigued fituation fhe was in, it
was no little chagrin to the General, that
he could afford her no affiftance to cheer
up her fpirits for fuch an undertaking; he
had not even a cup of wine to offer her—
but from a foldier's wife fhe obtained a
little rum and dirty water! With this poor
refrefhment fhe fet out in an open boat,
which was furnifhed by the General, with
a few lines of recommendation to General
Gates, for his protection. The Chaplain
that officiated at General Frafer's funeral
undertook to accompany her, and with her
waiting-maid, and the Major's *valet de
chambre* (who then had a ball in his fhoulder, which he received in the late action,

in

in fearching for the Major after he was wounded) fhe rowed down the river to meet the enemy.——But to return to the army.

It was not till after day-light, on the morning of the 10th, that the artillery and the laft of the troops paffed the Fifh-Kill, and took pofition upon the heights and in the redoubts we had formerly conftructed. On our arrival at Saratoga, a corps of the enemy, between five and fix hundred, were difcovered throwing up intrenchments on the heights, but upon our approach re-tired over the ford of the Hudfon's river, and joined a body pofted to oppofe our paffage there.

A detachment of artificers, under a ftrong efcort, were fent to repair bridges, and open a road on the weft fide of the river to Fort Edward; but the enemy being ftrongly pofted on the heights of the Fifh-Kill,

Kill, and making a difpofition to give us battle, that efcort was recalled. The Provincials who were left to cover the artificers, upon a very flight attack ran away, leaving them to efcape as they could, without a poffibility of their performing any work.

While thefe different movements were carrying on, the *batteaux* with provifions were frequently fired upon from the oppofite fide of the river, fome of them were loft, and feveral men killed and wounded in thofe that remained.

On the 11th the enemy continued the attacks upon the *batteaux*, feveral were taken and retaken, but their fituation being nearer to the main force of the enemy than to ours, it was judged neceffary to land the provifions, and fend them up the hill, as it was impoffible to fecure them by any other means : this was effected

under

under a heavy fire, and with the greateſt difficulty.

The intentions of the enemy became now very apparent, and no doubt General Gates thought he ſhould be able to gain more advantage from the ſituation and circumſtances of our army, by cutting off our proviſions, and otherwiſe harraſſing and diſtreſſing us, by the galling fire of the riflemen, who were every where placed about in the woods, than by giving us battle, and running the chance of a victory.

The poſſible means of farther retreat were conſidered in a council of war, compoſed of the General officers; and the only one that ſeemed expedient, or in the leaſt practicable, was attended with ſuch danger, as afforded little hopes of ſucceſs, but nevertheleſs the reſolve was it ſhould be attempted. This was by a night march to Fort Edward,

ward, the troops carrying their provifions on their backs, leaving artillery, baggage, and other incumbrances behind, and to force a paffage at the ford, either above or below that fort.

While the army were preparing for this bold and refolute undertaking, fome fcouts returned with intelligence, that the enemy were ftrongly intrenched oppofite thofe fords, and poffeffed a camp in force on the high grounds, between Fort Edward and Fort George, with cannon; exclufive of which, they had parties down the whole fhore to watch our motions, and fome pofts fo near us, on our fide of the water, that it was impoffible the army could make the leaft motion without being difcovered.

Notwithftanding the number of the Americans, which was hourly increafing, General Gates acted with as much precaution as if the fuperiority was on our fide,

as

as the ground where he encamped was,
from its nature and the works he had
thrown up, inattackable.

Our march to Fort Edward being thus
prevented, the army was posted as well as
the ground would admit of, fortifying our
camp, and preparing for any attempt that
the enemy, from our reduced state, might
be induced to make.

The state and situation of our army was
truly calamitous!—Worn down by a series
of inceffant toils and stubborn actions;
abandoned in our utmost distrefs by the
Indians; weakened by the desertion, and
disappointed as to the efficacy of the Canadians and Provincials, by their timidity;
the regular troops reduced, by the late
heavy loffes of many of our best men and
distinguished officers, to only 3500 effective
men, of which number there were not
quite 2000 British:—in this state of weak-
nefs

nefs, no poffibility of retreat, our provifions nearly exhaufted, and invefted by an
army of four times our number, that
almoft encircled us, who would not attack
us from a knowledge of our fituation, and
whofe works could not be affaulted in any
part. In this perilous fituation the men
lay continually upon their arms, the enemy
inceffantly cannonading us, and their rifle
and cannon fhot reaching every part of our
camp.

True courage fubmits with great difficulty to defpair, and in the midft of all
thofe dangers and arduous trials, the
valor and conftancy of the Britifh troops
were aftonifhing: they ftill retained their
fpirits, in hopes that either the long-
expected relief would arrive from New-
York, which the army implicitly believed,
from an order that had been given out at
our camp at Still-Water, ftating that powerful armies were to act in co-operation
with

with ours, or that the enemy would attack us, which was moft fervently wifhed for, as it would have given us an opportunity of dying gallantly, or extricating ourfelves with honor.

After waiting the whole of the 13th day of October, in anxious expectation of what it would produce, and to which time it had been refolved to endure all extremities in maintaining our ground againft the enemy—no profpect of affiftance appearing, and no rational ground of hope remaining, it was thought proper, in the evening, to take an exact account of the provifions left, which amounted to no more than three days fhort allowance.

In this ftate of diftrefs, a council of war was called, to which all the Generals, Field-officers, and commanding-officers of corps were fummoned, when it was unanimoufly agreed, that in the prefent circumftances

we

we could do no other than treat with the enemy.

Ernesto Gates

Overtures were accordingly propofed to General Gates, who harfhly rejected them, reminding us of our enervated ftate, from a toilfome campaign, diminifhed numbers, fcanty fubfiftence, and the impoffibility of frefh fupply. Thefe reafons were urged on the fpur of the moment, minute confideration denied, and a decifive anfwer required. We felt their force, but compliance was never thought of, it would have too feverely wounded the dignity of our military character.

The refufal of our overtures was mortifying in the extreme, yet inftead of depreffing, it raifed our magnanimity; the interval of fufpence, indeed, difturbed our repofe; anxiety was awake to confequences— ftill we adhered to our purpofe with manly firmnefs. A ftate of fufpence, to a reflecting

ing mind, is worfe than death; that was our ftate till the convention was finally adjufted.

The obftacles to the accomplifhment of the convention at firft appeared infurmountable, for General Gates conceived that our complicated embarraffments fufficiently juftified him, according to the rules of war, in infifting on an unconditional furrender of the army: they were difdainfully rejected, and he was peremptorily informed, that notwithftanding our reduced numbers, if he ftill perfifted, our final appeal fhould be to the fword, as the Britifh troops would rufh upon the enemy, determined to give no quarter.

General Gates, from having been once in our fervice, was fully convinced of what exertions Britifh troops were capable, in any dangerous emergency; he was therefore quickly fenfible of the impolicy of

H h coercion,

coercion, and with very great prudence declined hazarding a frefh conflict with men who preferred death to a difgraceful fubmiffion. Awed by our firmnefs, he retracted his demands, and honorable terms were granted; the particulars, as they are undoubtedly in the Gazette, I fhall of courfe pafs over.

To a reverfe of fortune we yielded with becoming dignity, but our honor was fafe, and equanimity of temper marked our cha-racter, even in adverfity.

General Burgoyne has done every thing in this convention for the good of the troops, confiftent with the fervice of his King and country: all that wifdom, valor, and a ftrict fenfe of honor could fuggeft. Confident, no doubt, of having exerted himfelf with indefatigable fpirit in their fervice, he will defpife popular clamor, truly fenfible that no perfect and unbiaffed judge

of

of actual fervice can condemn him.   Addi-
fon has fomewhere obferved,

" 'Tis not in mortals to command fuccefs !"

And as the populace, in this verfatile
age ftartle at untoward events, fo our General is liable to be expofed to public cen-
fure.   Ample juftice muft raife him in the
mind of every liberal man who will judge
with caution, acquit him with honor, and
take him to his heart as the foldier's
friend——as a man of cool judgment, but
ardent for glory——as courageous but unfortunate !

END OF THE FIRST VOLUME.

DATE DUE